DATE DUE			

Making Sense of the Men in Your Life

What Makes Them Tick, What Ticks You Off, and How to Live in Harmony

Dr. Kevin Leman

NELSON BOOKS
A Division of Thomas Nelson Publishers
Since 1798

www.thomasnelson.com

Published in Nashville, Tennessee, by Thomas Nelson, Inc.

Some names of persons used in this book are fictionalized to protect the privacy of the individuals.

Library of Congress Cataloging-in-Publication Date

Leman, Kevin.

Making sense of the men in your life : what makes them tick, what ticks you off, and how to live in harmony / Kevin Leman.

p. cm.

ISBN 0-8407-3494-8 (hc)

1. Men—Psychology. 2. Sex differences (Psychology). 3. Man-woman relationships. 4. Man-woman relationships—Religious aspects—Christianity. I. Title.

HQ1090 .L46 2001

305.31—dc21 00-046538

CIP

Printed in the United States of America

7 8 9 10 QW 06 05 04

To my son, Kevin Anderson Leman II
You are the best son, and you'll be a great husband and dad
someday. God has given you such a wonderfully creative
and delightful sense of humor. May you always use your talent
and imagination wisely to help and encourage others.
As Dorothy Gish said, "Son . . . you've got it!"
I love you very much.
Your dad

Books by Dr. Kevin Leman

Among Dr. Leman's twenty-two titles are the following books:

Bringing Up Kids Without Tearing Them Down
Living in a Stepfamily Without Getting Stepped On
Unlocking the Secrets of Your Childhood Memories
What a Difference a Daddy Makes

Contents

1. What Is It About Men? 1

Part 1: How Did God Fit So Much Testosterone into Such a Tiny Body? 15

2. The Boy Your Husband Once Was (and in Many Ways Still Is) 17
3. What Is It About Boys and Sex? 43

Part 2: The Man Who Matters Most 55

4. Why You Married the Man You Married. 57
5. Coming to Grips with Father Hunger. 71
6. A Daughter's Self-Defense. 93
7. The Strong Man Stumbles 105

Part 3: Your Husband: He Can Be Handy Around the House, but I'm Not Sure He Goes with the Furniture 115

8. Give Him Some Credit . . . and Some Time! 117
9. A Man's Best Friend Is Not a Dog. 129
10. Sexual Fulfillment 145
11. Communicating with Your Man 175
12. A Man and His Ego. 187

Part 4: Men You Don't Have to Live With (but Who Still Drive You Crazy) 201

13. Men at Work. 203
14. Single Issues: Life As a Single or Newly Divorced Woman 219
15. Questions About Men in General 235

Epilogue: The Pesky Duck *243*
Notes *247*
About the Author *249*

What Is It About Men?

Are you willing to take a test to find out just how much you know (or don't know) about males (boys and men)? Get out your pen and see if you can correctly answer the following:

- What is the most important need in a married man's life?
  a. Sex
  b. Admiration
  c. Food
  d. The remote control
  e. Golf
  f. Watching sports on television
  g. Money
  h. None of the above
  [Letter *b* is the right answer. See Chapter 10.]

- Your husband is hopelessly lost on a trip. He refuses to stop and ask for directions because
  a. It's beneath him to ask.
  b. It goes against his stubborn nature.
  c. He's too proud to acknowledge he's lost.
  d. He loves the challenge of figuring it out.
  e. It's a macho thing.
  f. None of the above.
  [Hint: "None of the above" is the right answer again! See Chapter 12 for the right one.]

- More than 80 percent of Christian women will violate their marriage vows in the coming week. True or false?
  [The correct answer is "true," but how? See Chapter 12.]

- What is the most important thing a female employee wears in the workplace?
  [See Chapter 13.]

- What do 96 percent of boys do that most mothers don't want to know about?
  [See Chapter 3.]

- How often do you think a man thinks about sex?
  a. The same amount as a woman
  b. Twice as much as a woman
  c. Five times as much as a woman
  d. Ten times as much as a woman
  e. Thirty-three times as much as a woman
  [See Chapter 9.]

- ✦ What do you need to do before your dad dies?
  [See Chapter 6.]

- ✦ Why did you marry the man you married?
  [See Chapter 4.]

In this book, I'm going to break down the doors and throw open the windows to give you an up-close and personal look at how the "other half" thinks, feels, and behaves. For instance, when your husband wakes up in the morning, what's really going on in his mind? When your son closes the door of his bedroom in the afternoon, what's he doing? When your father looks at you as an adult woman/daughter, what conflicting emotions is he experiencing? When your male boss or subordinate finds out how competent you are, what's he likely to do?

You may not like everything you read in this book, but you'd better pay attention to it. Your ability to succeed in the workplace, for instance, will require you to learn how to get along with men—even if all of them don't respect you. Your ability to succeed in marriage will depend in large part upon your understanding of what makes a husband feel fulfilled. And your skill as a mother will require that you learn to appreciate what makes a boy a boy.

Without this knowledge, how are you ever going to beat the odds? Let's take marriage as an example. Does it scare you at all when I ask, "How will you stay married when so many women get divorced?" What makes you so different from the tens of thousands of other sincere, loving women who get married, fully intending that they will die married, only to suffer the heart-wrenching breakup of a marriage that dies long before they do?

Don't think that you're immune to the possibility of divorce just because you're a Christian. Perhaps you didn't realize that *Christians are more likely to experience divorce than non-Christians.* That's right. According to research conducted by the Barna organization, while about 24 percent of American adults have experienced at least one divorce, 27 percent of self-described born-again Christians are currently or have previously been divorced. Barna noted, "Because of the large sample size involved, that difference is statistically significant."[1]

Barna discovered that educational achievement, household income, and political ideology are unrelated to divorce. Far more dangerous, maritally speaking (at least, according to the statistics), is being a "nondenominational Protestant"; a whopping 34 percent of them have experienced divorce. In fact, Barna reported that atheists and agnostics fare much better in marriage than do Baptists—suffering a 21 percent divorce rate versus a 29 percent divorce rate, respectively.

What's so different about you? How are you going to be different and keep your marriage together? How do I know you won't end up in my office desperately trying to hold your marriage together after an affair? You may answer, "You don't understand, Dr. Leman. My husband and I are deeply, *deeply* in love. We'd never get a divorce." Here is my response: "Do you think a man and a woman begin their romance by saying, 'I'll have my lawyer contact your lawyer'? A man and a woman walk down the aisle for a marriage ceremony after declaring their deep, *deep* love for each other."

Do you want to die married? If you do, are you willing to invest the time it will take to read this book and learn what's really going on in your husband's mind?

Here's the first insider's secret of this book: One of the best things you can do to give your marriage longevity is to learn more about how a man thinks and feels. A man likes a woman who knows how a man thinks and feels. A man feels much more at home with such a woman.

He'll be more relaxed and probably much better at growing in his understanding of what she wants.

> **Leman's Law #1:**
>
> Men like women who know how a man thinks and feels.

I wish every wife in this country would read a letter that appeared in a column by Ann Landers. A woman wrote to Ann after having an affair with a coworker, signing her name "Smart Too Late."

"At first," Smart Too Late wrote, "it was just flirting, but before long, we knew we were in love. We finally decided to divorce our spouses and get married."

Less than two years later, the woman lamented, "What do I have today? My two children are now in therapy, and I have huge legal bills. My in-laws despise me because they see their grandchildren only twice a year."

And the new hubby, the one she fell "in love" with? "[He] sits in a chair at night drinking beer and smoking cigarettes while I cook, clean, and fold laundry." She then added something profound: "*I wish I had used the effort I spent trying to hide my affair and put it to work saving my first marriage. I would have been a lot happier.*"[2]

Are you willing to spend a few hours learning how to make your husband *really* happy? It's not too late if you're still married!

Again, you may not like everything I tell you, but I guarantee you this—you're getting it straight. This is what most men talk about. Granted, not all men are alike, but taken as a whole, they are much more similar to each other than they are to women. Knowing a few basic principles about how men are wired will go a long way toward helping you have far more satisfying relationships with them.

If you really want to get along with men and boys, the first thing you must accept is that all across this country, males are redrawing a line that you must never try to erase.

Drawing the Line

Over the past several decades, our culture has cleverly redefined men's roles. The new "sensitive" man is supposed to be able to read a woman's mind (somehow picking up a woman's intuition) and prefer to spend an evening cuddling and talking.

An evening of cuddling and talking is about as unnatural for a man as it would be for a fish to climb a tree. When men get together, we talk about our jobs, the bills, the weather, the stock market, and the local sports team—anything that's one step removed from "us." When a buddy tells us his wife just had a baby, we congratulate him, but we usually don't ask, "Okay, how much did the baby weigh?"

"Nine pounds? Are you kidding me? That's a huge baby! Now, how long was he? Twenty-two inches? The size of a nice walleye! Okay, tell me about the labor—how many hours until transition?"

That's just not us! Odds are, we'll forget to ask whether it was a boy or a girl unless our friend volunteers the information.

Another thing women just don't understand is what it means when I say that men are physical beings. We are *attracted* to the physical. This is true even of men who don't take care of themselves physically. I'm not trying to shock you here, but I want to open up your eyes to a truth that often gets glossed over. I want you to think of a man you most admire and trust, and he must be a nonrelative. (I guarantee you don't want to hear this, but I will tell it to you anyway.) You got this guy in your mind? Good. Now put yourself in a position where you're meeting this man in a social situation. In less than one-fifth of a second, this man has checked you out from your toes to your head and *all* major spots in between.

Don't believe me? Ask your husband. Perhaps you'll believe him.

If we're honorable men, we won't mentally undress you. We won't imagine doing things with you that should be done only with our wives, but we will *notice* you. That's the way we're wired. We don't mean to offend you. We can learn not to leer or to make crude remarks. But most of us look.

I heard of a woman at a Bible study who actually insisted that if her husband was "truly godly," a naked woman should be able to walk through the room and sit in his lap and he wouldn't be *tempted* to look. I'm sorry, but that's not gonna happen!

Ladies, with all due apologies, I think I'm speaking for a lot of your husbands, sons, and fathers when I say I'm drawing the line. I'm not going to any more Tupperware parties. I won't eat quiche. I won't apologize for thinking that sex and football are two of God's and man's greatest inventions (respectively). I might even stop this afternoon at a red light and pick my nose for a while.

I'm sick of getting in touch with my "feminine self." I like the masculine part just fine, thank you very much. There are some parts of my "masculine" body that I'm completely enamored with and proud of. I'm sorry if my comments offend you, but I know that a growing cadre of men are fed up trying to be something they're not.

For several decades now, some of the more ridiculous members of our society have been trying to argue that there is no real difference between men and women. Testosterone and estrogen, in their view, have far less impact than cultural conditioning. Sometimes, they go to absurd lengths to establish this point. FIFA, soccer's international governing body, funded a two-year exhaustive study that enabled the researchers to conclude that yes, men play soccer far more roughly than women do.[3] No kidding!

Our first lesson is this: *Don't fault your man for being a man.* Testosterone has its advantages. How else do you think we get those mayonnaise jars open? But with the advantages come the "disadvantages" (speaking from a woman's perspective). Your husband, son, and father probably think about sex far more than you realize—or maybe care to know. On the other hand, we're never going to catch up with you in the sheer volume of words you produce. And on the opening day of deer season, we may have a difficult time thinking about our jobs, our wives, or our children. Instead, there's a distant glow in our eyes as we focus our entire energy on one goal: "Kill Bambi!"

If you try to raise your son exactly the same way you raise your daughter, you're inviting disaster. Boys have wildly different attention spans, for instance, preferring to look at objects for shorter (but more active) periods of time than girls do. In other words, they are far more intense and far more quickly bored. Their brains are wired so that they need to move rapidly from object to object in space. They take in less sensory information than girls do (the same is true for men—which explains why your husband didn't notice the new haircut or the new wallpaper!), have three times more reading difficulties than girls do, and often come into their verbal skills almost a year later than girls do.[4]

Your son is not going to be like your daughter, and your husband is not going to be like your college roommate. If you try to turn your husband into your lifelong best girlfriend, you'll be forever frustrated. If you wish your dad was as easy to talk to as your mother, you're being unrealistic.

Men are different, and frankly we *like* being different. I like not having to gather a group of reinforcements to back me up so that I can visit the men's room in a restaurant. I'm perfectly happy going there by myself. And I'm sure *you're* perfectly happy being able to watch a television show without continually surfing all the other channels just to see what's on.

In an honorable struggle to gain more respect for women, we've thrown out common sense with our prejudice. Clearly men and women are of equal social value; men aren't worth more than women; God doesn't love men more than women or women more than men. (For that matter, God doesn't love adults more than children, or whites more than nonwhites, or Protestants more than non-Protestants.) But someone took this notion of social equality and came up with this ridiculous conclusion: "Therefore, men and women are the same."

That's where we went awry, because men and women are not the same. Our brains are different; our body chemicals are very different; we see life from completely different angles. For example, an article in the December 1999 issue of the journal *Cerebral Cortex* reported that the part of the brain controlling visual-spatial abilities and concepts of "mental space"—skills necessary for tasks such as mathematics and architecture—is about 6 percent larger in men than in women.[5] Men's brains are larger, but women's brains contain more brain cells.[6]

Women's hearts beat faster than men's hearts. When men and women perform identical tasks, different areas of their brains light up in response.[7]

Have you wondered how your husband can work so long and so hard? Well, studies have now shown that women have more severe and longer-lasting pain than men[8] (but you already knew that, didn't you?). On average, you experience headaches, facial and oral pain, back pain, and other ailments more frequently and more severely than does your husband.

Although a few researchers still try to pretend that women's and men's bodies are essentially the same outside the bikini lines, more and more doctors and scientists are coming into agreement with the view of Dr. Marianne Legato at Columbia University, who says, "We're talking about substantive, important differences between men and women in every system of the body, from the central nervous system to the gut, to the skin, to the way in which we metabolize drugs."[9]

These differences affect every area of marital life. For instance, about 31 percent of men experience sexual difficulty, compared to 43 percent (getting dangerously close to half!) of women.[10] One study found that one out of every three women said she was uninterested in sex, whereas only one out of every six men said the same thing. And one out of every ten men reported that sex provides little pleasure for him, but one out of every five women admitted that sex isn't any fun![11] That's understandable, considering that it is extremely rare for men to be incapable of achieving orgasm, yet between 20 and 30 percent of women consistently struggle in this regard.

The nature of sexual desire is equally distinct. You're probably not surprised that researchers have found that, yes, a man's sexual desire is "more easily triggered by external cues" and (I can hear many women sighing already) is "more constant across the life cycle."[12] (That's a fancy way of saying your man will, on average, be easily aroused until the day he stops breathing!) The same study indicated that a woman's sexual desire is much more "reflective" and "reactive" to her partner rather than being spontaneous or initiated by her. In other words, her desire grows in interaction with her partner, while her husband's desire grows merely by seeing his wife (or any woman, for that matter) naked.

Because we men are so different from you, you can't expect to just "know" how to love your man, raise your boy, or relate to your dad.

We're foreign creatures, oddballs, and utter mysteries. The purpose of this book is to help you understand how different males are and provide you with workable strategies so that you can better relate to us.

Vive La Différence!

Rather than trying to turn men into women or women into men, why don't we take a step back and say, "Thank God, we're different!" In celebration of these differences, I'd like to showcase some of the things you'll *never* hear in a typical marriage.

- A wife saying, "Honey, I hope you don't mind, but I splurged to get the NFL package on cable so that you can watch more football in our bedroom."
- A husband saying, "Let's just cuddle and talk tonight—no sex, okay?"
- A wife saying, "Buy more shoes? Why would I buy more shoes? I already have two pairs!"
- A husband saying, "Hey, why don't we rent a nice romantic comedy video tonight?"
- A wife saying, "I know we had sex this morning, but I just can't get enough of you. Why don't we forget the dirty dishes and the laundry that needs to be done and spend the rest of the evening making mad, passionate love—again!"
- A husband saying, "Honey, is there anything I can do to encourage your mother to stay with us longer than a month this summer?"

- A wife saying, "Don't worry about doing anything for our anniversary. It's no big deal."
- A husband saying, "Nah, forget the baseball game. Let's go shopping all day long!"

If any of these comments bring a smile to your face, then you probably realize there is more you can learn about the roughly 49 percent of our population that is fueled by testosterone.

Where We're Headed

This book is presented in four parts, according to chronological order. First, I'll introduce you to the world of boys. You may not have a son, but I want to help you better understand your husband by helping you understand the boy that he was (and in many ways still is).

Next, we'll consider why you married the man you married by looking at the man who profoundly imprinted you early in life. I'm speaking, of course, about your father. It's my goal to help you understand yourself better and to learn how to navigate the choppy waters of adult father-daughter relationships. The good news is, dads change as they get older. If you know *how* they change, you may be able to initiate a far more meaningful and deeper relationship with the man who has probably perplexed you for most of your life.

After that, we'll dive into the world of husbands. In my practice I've found that women's ignorance of men is exceeded only by men's ignorance of women. I continue to be amazed that a couple can live in the same house for ten, fifteen, even twenty years and still not realize what is most important to each other.

In the fourth part, we'll deal with a particularly touchy issue: men you don't have to live with but who still drive you crazy. We'll begin by discussing men at work. You get to choose your husband, but you may be stuck with your boss and occasionally a subordinate. How can a woman survive and thrive in a world that was dominated by men just a few decades ago? We'll also talk about how you can relate to an ex-husband or to single men in a dating relationship.

Ready to jump in? Let's go!

Part 1

How Did God Fit So Much Testosterone into Such a Tiny Body?

The Boy Your Husband Once Was (and in Many Ways Still Is)

My wife, Sande, picked me up from work one evening so that we could go out to dinner. We left my car at the office, and since Sande was already behind the wheel, she started driving our minivan down Broadway.

Broadway is a six-lane highway (three lanes on each side). To the female mind, it provides a comforting array of choices. The safest bet is the right lane. That's usually the slowest lane, but it keeps you from the precarious middle, from which you can be assaulted by accidents on either side.

To the male mind, three lanes represent a complex web of competition. The middle lane is often the best one to drive in because if you get caught behind someone who is going slowly, you can slide to the left or right—in essence, you double your options of getting ahead and winning the race.

It dawned on me, however, that Sande was completely clueless to the fact that a race was going on. She drove in the comfortable right lane—the one closest to the sidewalk—and gently pulled up to a stoplight behind a long array of vehicles. And then she did the most curious thing of all.

She just sat there; she didn't look around her.

That's when it hit me. She wasn't competing!

"Uh, Sande," I said, "let me ask you something. Do you *ever* count cars when you come to a red light?"

Sande looked at me as if I was from Pluto. "Why would I count cars?"

I decided to delight her with my comprehensive awareness of the situation. "We're in the right lane, seated behind ten cars, a bus, and a dump truck. The middle lane has two cars. The lead car is a Mercedes and the second car is a BMW—both of which have superb acceleration. The outside lane isn't such a safe bet. It has three cars in it, but two of them are minivans, and they might try to turn left at the next light." Confident that Sande was impressed with my grasp of our dire circumstances, I stopped talking.

She said, "So?"

"*So*?" I shot back. "Why aren't you in the middle lane?"

"I'm very happy where I am."

I threw up my hands. "You'll never win the race in this lane."

"What are you talking about?" she replied.

Sande had no idea what I was getting at. She didn't realize that we should have been trying to put more cars behind us than allowing cars to pass us. All these years she's been driving, she's been oblivious that close to 50 percent of the population has been racing against her while she has been puttering along in the right-hand lane!

A big challenge in a marriage is learning to understand someone who is so very different from you. Part of the problem is that a man thinks he understands a woman, and a woman thinks she understands a man. I want to let you in on a little secret: *You don't understand your husband nearly as well as you think you do.*

If you want to test me on this, go ahead. Write down a list of what you think is most important to your husband, including how you assume he most wants to be loved. Chances are, even if you've read all the James Dobson and Gary Smalley books, you're going to get it wrong. The problem is not with Dobson and Smalley, who are great communicators (and good friends of mine), but the information seems so foreign and bizarre to you as a woman *that you just can't believe it could be true*. Even after you read it in print, you struggle to understand a man's true priorities.

This misunderstanding arises in part because girls often think boys are just like them—except for the outdoor plumbing. As a woman, you probably have little idea of what life is like for a little boy, which isn't surprising. You've never been one, after all! Yet your husband's experience as a little boy has had a profound impact on who he is now as a man. The way his mother treated him, the way his male peers did (or did not) respect him, and the way others looked down on him—all combined to help create the man you married.

Consequently, I think it's wise to introduce you to your husband *before he hit puberty*. Just what was your man like as a little boy? You may not want to go here, but understand this: Virtually everything I say about boys is also true about men. We males might change our shoe size, but the very qualities that make boys boys also make men men. If you have a son, these chapters will help you to understand him better. If you are a Sunday school or elementary school teacher, you will be better able to relate to the boys in your class. But the primary purpose is to know the little boy inside your husband.

Leman's Law #2:

Men are basically little boys who wear bigger shoes.

I was reminded of how much alike men and boys are when a friend told me about shopping on the Internet for his son's Christmas present. He knew his boy wanted a R.A.D. robot, so he looked it up on a site that carries comments from satisfied buyers. One eleven-year-old boy gave the robot high marks, gloating, "R.A.D. is rad! I scared my sister, shot her cat in the butt, and stole my dad's glasses. R.A.D. rules!"

What caught my friend's attention was that a similar review was written by one of two dads: "Cool! Even if the TV remote is on the other couch, I can use this robot to get it for me. I'll never have to get up again. I can chase my kids around the house with this too. I can also shoot the darts at my wife while she does the dishes. WOW!"

The boy uses the robot to scare his sister, chase the family pet, and steal things from his dad. The dad uses it to chase his kids and pester his wife. Testosterone is testosterone, whether it's packed inside a tiny little body or one with a bulging belly.

Tiny Testosterone

One of the toughest acts to play on earth is being a boy between the ages of eight and fifteen. By the time he is eight years old, a boy is no longer considered cute and certainly not adorable. If your husband was anything like me, he probably looked a little funny, maybe even a little creepy.

Have you ever noticed how body parts grow at different speeds?

Ears can overtake the head, for instance, or the head can overtake the body, creating a truly comical character. Not to mention the damage that a well-placed zit can do to any young adolescent's self-esteem.

While such a boy is too big to be adorable, he's too little to get any respect. He doesn't have biceps to speak of, so older boys will push him around. He is slowly, painfully changing from a boy into a man, so he is struggling with a Porsche-size engine in the body of a Hot Wheels car.

> **Leman's Law #3:**
> One of the toughest acts to play on earth is being a boy between the ages of eight and fifteen.

But then it happened. Your husband woke up one day around seventh or eighth grade and found his first pubic or chest hair, but it probably wasn't soon enough (or thick enough) to keep him from humiliation in the school showers. There the older, fully haired, fully developed Neanderthals snickered at the, ahem, less-than-gigantic proportions of Johnny's little jimmy.

It's gotten a little better. Back in my day, we boys had to swim in the nude during gym class. When I think of the most frightening aspects of my life, swimming *au naturelle* is definitely in the top five.

A guy in my class named Alan was huge—in every significant place! He was a *man!* Even by the seventh grade, Alan's legs had hair on them.

Guess who had to stand right next to Alan in line? Little Kevin Leman, whose skinny white body had a sum total of one hair—a little spaghetti noodle that I was tempted to darken with a felt-tipped pen so that everybody could see it. I looked down below my waist and, well, let's just say that Alan looked every bit a man and I was every bit a boy.

In a recently built high school, the boys' locker room has open showers, which has been the typical design for years, but the girls' locker room has single shower stalls with curtains. Your husband never had this protection, and when a boy doesn't develop as fast as his peers, he can't hide. He's going to be ridiculed, and that hurts.

Not only are boys often underdeveloped, but some of us are just plain stupid. In my much younger years, I was eating spaghetti at my mom's friend's house when I passed on the sauce in favor of the butter.

"Kevin," my mom's friend said, "you should have some sauce. It'll put hair on your chest."

That's all I needed to hear. I piled enough sauce on top of those noodles to drown a small rat!

That night, as I got ready for bed, I pulled back my pajamas just as my mom walked into the room.

"Kevin, what are you doing?"

"I'm looking for the hair."

My mom had a great laugh, and I had one of the most humiliating moments of my life.

Preadolescence is a tough, tough time. If your husband was the typical boy, he probably received neither affection nor respect. He was too big to be cuddled in public, but too small to be respected by those just slightly older than he was.

To make matters more difficult, your husband might have grown up feeling guilty for being male. Just a couple of decades ago, when your spouse might have been a boy, actor Alan Alda openly talked about "testosterone poisoning," as if to be male was to be the carrier of a latent disease. Remember those days when many feminists declared virtual war against all things male—and many "sensitive" men joined them in heaping abuse on the "poison" of testosterone?

The crescendo is building today as boys are being blamed for every girl's failure. The American Association of University Women (AAUW) sponsored a study of female-only classrooms. Much to its surprise and chagrin, the AAUW found that single-sex classrooms improved the academic marks of a few girls but by no means improved the scores of all. Columnist Kathleen Parker points out that hidden underneath this study is a pernicious, antiboy assumption: "Missing entirely from the discussion is whether single-sex classes might be beneficial to boys. Why? Because nobody cares. It's easier to find Waldo's red-striped shirt in an American flag factory than it is to find concern for boys in a sampling of news stories about the AAUW study."[1]

She continues, "You'd think boys were some sort of toxin polluting the air, the elimination of which would enhance girls' brain function. Toxic is the assumption that boys are privileged oppressors of girls; pollution is what we're doing to the hearts and minds of a generation of boys and girls who are being trained to consider one another the enemy."

Ever since a study found that teachers call on boys more than girls in math classes, boys have become "the enemy" in many feminists' minds. That's why the women naturally assumed that if they could get the boys out of the way—freeing females from the barbaric "testosterone terrorists"—the girls' scores would go through the roof.

Parker talks about how one of her boys was forced to put up with a teacher who refuses to use generic male pronouns. It's not that she occasionally replaces *he* with *she*; it's that she *always* refers to *she* instead of *he*. Writes Parker, "I thought, this is going to be a tough year for the boys. It has been."

The truth is, as Parker indicates, boys get lower grades than girls (even though their scores on standardized tests tend to be higher). But more seriously, boys have a suicide rate five times higher than that of girls, and boys are diagnosed with learning disabilities at a rate six times higher than that of girls.

Parker concludes, "Bet your hacienda on this: Were girls committing suicide and suffering learning disabilities at the rate boys are, we'd be throwing money at researchers like rice on newlyweds."

Does any reasonable person doubt what Parker says?

I meet many adult men today who still carry shame and guilt over how they "underperformed" as boys. Since most of them grew up in an age when learning disabilities were not recognized as such, many husbands have grown up feeling just plain dumb, and they often act reserved because they have learned it is better to be quiet and left alone than to speak up and be laughed at.

And men who didn't underperform may carry the baggage of being male. I know of a very competent firstborn mid-level executive (now in his early forties) who was pulled aside by his boss and told, "Listen, Jim, I'm sorry to tell you this, but you were hired about ten years too late. Top management has made it clear that the company leadership needs to become much more diverse. Given the fact that you're a man and that you're white, you've already got two strikes against you."

This same attitude—reverse discrimination, so to speak—is being lobbed at males at all levels. The educational system has plenty of wonderful, caring teachers (my daughter is one of them!), but it is also littered with feminists who see a boy and immediately think, *We have seen the enemy and he's wearing a jockstrap.*

Why Does My Husband Act Like . . . a Man?

One of my funniest moments in therapy occurred when a woman started complaining to me about her husband. "I just don't understand him," she said, describing many perfectly normal male traits. "Why does my husband act so much like . . . like . . ."

"A man?" I suggested.

"That's it!"

If you're a woman who, like this one, never had any brothers, your husband is more than likely a complete mystery to you at times. The following information may seem elementary to you, but if you were seldom around boys, let's get a few basic understandings down on paper. Boys (and men) are competitive, they like goofy things, and they like to play rough.

Boys Are Competitive

While girls frequently huddle in groups on the playground and discuss who's most popular and similar topics, the boys probably argue over who won the last competition. By nature, boys are competitive. They want to win. It doesn't matter whether they're playing a game of Monopoly, tossing around a basketball, or trying to stomp on and kill the highest number of ants. They usually want to be the best. When they grow up and get a driver's license, they naturally begin counting the number of cars they pass on the way to work; they also compare salaries and the sizes of their offices. Males never really stop competing.

Young coaches quickly catch on to this competitive nature. It's one thing to give a boys' sports team a drill, but if you really want to ratchet up the intensity, make the drill competitive—put half of the team against the other half. *Then* you'll see the boys give their best.

A city in the Pacific Northwest decided competition among younger boys was "a bad influence," so the coaches decided to stop keeping score at baseball games. They asked the boys to play their best, and then afterward, when the boys asked who won, they were told, "It doesn't matter as long as you played your hardest."

The experiment never worked because many of the boys kept their own score. They cared about winning and losing—and why shouldn't they? One of the most important lessons in life is learning how to lose, get up, and keep going. Many of these same boys will be applying for jobs where only one out of ten or even one out of a thousand people will be chosen. They need to learn how to compete, do their best, and face either the pleasure of accomplishment or the pain of falling short.

Competition is one reason that Pokémon cards have been so wildly popular with boys. Essentially (beyond all the controversy) Pokémon is going to war with cards; it feeds into a young boy's sense of empowerment, particularly how a character can evolve into a more powerful one.

The competitive nature of boys is such that brothers will fight to the death over unsolvable disputes—who gets the last piece of pie, who gets to put in the last piece of the jigsaw puzzle, whether or not the runner was tagged out in a game of baseball. Your husband grew up in this world, always fighting for his "fair share."

I heard of one hilarious—and typically male—incident when a mother caught her two boys arguing over who would get the first pancake. The mother thought she had a golden opportunity to provide a moral lesson, so she said, "If Jesus were sitting here, He would say, 'Let My brother have the first pancake. I can wait.'" The older son turned to his brother and said, "Ryan, you be Jesus."

Boys Like Goofy Things

My mom hated doing my laundry, and who could blame her? One time she reached into my pants pocket and got bitten.

"*Keevvviin!*" she screamed. "*Get down here right now!*"

From the way she yelled, I assumed somebody died. "Yeah, Mom, what is it?"

"*What* is in your pocket?"

I fished in my jeans and pulled out a crayfish, a cricket, two salamanders, and a grasshopper.

"Bait," I said proudly. "I went fishing today, remember?"

My mom probably wanted to strangle me, but she was a very patient woman. She said, "Fine, but next time you go fishing could you *please* remove all bugs, insects, and anything that's slimy and alive from your jeans before you put them in the wash for me to find?"

Then I went through my Milk-Bone stage. It takes a boy who watches his dog chewing on a Milk-Bone to think, *I wonder what that tastes like?* Worse, I found out I really *liked* the taste. Even more, I craved the attention eating the things brought to me, and I took pride in doing goofy things.

My mom never got used to this trick, but other people have. One Christmas, a woman who heard me talk on the radio sent me a box of *frosted* Milk-Bone dog biscuits. If they had invented those when I was a kid, I never would have eaten my dinner!

It wasn't long until my son paid me back. I was in my office many years ago when I got a frantic call from Sande. She was crying—in near hysterics—and I immediately felt my heart start to race. I was positive one of my kids was dead or at least critically injured.

"Honey, what's the matter?"

"It's Kevin!"

Oh, no! I thought. "Did he fall into the pool?"

"No," Sande said, "it's his pecker."

"His *pecker?*"

"Yeah, it's purple!"

"Purple? What happened? Did somebody hit him?"

"No, he colored it with a felt-tipped marker."

I burst out laughing. Little Kevin had always shown a predisposition toward art (art turned out to be Kevin's major in college), but this creative endeavor really beat them all.

"What are you laughing about?" Sande asked, horrified.

"That's the funniest thing I've ever heard!" I replied.

Because all of us men were once boys, we tend to have a good laugh rather than a good cry when it comes to our own boys' childhood pranks. Just because your husband has turned thirty doesn't mean he has lost his affinity for the goofy. We might have learned to regulate it a little bit better, but many of us still surprise our wives with the seemingly senseless things we do. If you gave me a Milk-Bone dog biscuit today, and I was in the right mood, I'd probably eat it (only Milk-Bone, by the way; no other brand will do!).

In this regard, I like to give wives the same advice I give concerned moms: Do yourself a favor and learn to laugh. Males do silly, goofy things. We always have, and we always will. With your husband and sons, you need to learn how to let boys be boys.

Boys Will Be Boys

I used to call my big brother "God." That was my nickname for him because that's the way he acted—as if he were accountable to no one but himself. He walked through the door, and I called out, "God's home."

He regularly pummeled me and on a whim would pound my shoulders into a pulp. I don't believe my brother is atypical. Males are far more likely to take out their tensions by using their fists. Your husband probably falls into one of two categories: he was beaten up, or he beat somebody else up.

A scar on my finger reminds me of the rough-and-tumble world of being a boy. The scar got there from Jimmy's teeth. Jimmy, a neighborhood kid, had the gall to say, "Your mom doesn't love you. Otherwise, she'd make you change out of your school clothes before you played."

In the next sixty seconds, Jimmy found out just how much my mother loved me, and his mother got to show *her* love by wiping the blood off Jimmy's nose and mouth.

Husbands get in an occasional tussle, too, which is rightly viewed as far more disturbing. Our "fights" tend to be more verbal. And just as schoolyard boys can make each other's nose bleed and then be best friends ten minutes later, we men can vehemently disagree over an issue, shout out all kinds of nasty things, come to an agreement, shake hands, and go play a round of golf—without seeing anything strange about the progression of events.

I don't advocate that mothers teach their boys to hit, nor do I suggest we turn a blind eye when boys fight. I am saying that a mother shouldn't act as if her boy is some unusual, homicidal maniac-in-training because he got into a schoolyard tussle or her husband is a "bad man" because he can become suddenly forceful.

You need to understand the world your husband grew up in. I remember how cruel we boys could be to each other. On one occasion, we tore the pants off a boy named Jimmy and gave him a "cherry belly." We spit on the guy's stomach and then slapped it until it became pink. We made him walk through a stretch of itch weed (remember, he wasn't wearing any pants) and forced him to climb a tree—*in the nude.*

If you talk with your husband and your father, I'll bet both of them can tell you similar stories. The details will be somewhat different, but boys have always mistreated other boys, and they probably always will. That's why men and women look at childhood pranks from two entirely different perspectives. The wife is thinking, *How could a boy be so cruel?* and the husband is thinking, *That reminds me of the time Charlie and I taught that Billy boy a lesson.*

You can have a fascinating talk with your husband tonight. Ask him if he was the one who was beaten up or the one who did the beating. Watch his eyes light up, and get ready to garner some new insights about why he is the way he is.

Affirmation of Maleness

Yet another provocative question will shed new light on your man: Was his mom comfortable with boys?

For your sake, I hope your husband's mom affirmed his maleness. The best way for a mother to do that is to tell a son what she appreciates about his dad and to praise the masculine qualities she wants her son to emulate. But in today's world, many moms are increasingly wary of affirming anything male because of their mistaken belief that sex roles are an artificial invention rather than a God-determined fact of life. Unfortunately, this social experiment doesn't produce tolerance or increased sensitivity. Instead, it creates confusion—and confused kids tend to make terrible choices.

I realize this is far from politically correct advice, but I don't want to play games with you. I have yet to meet a healthy woman who aspires to marry an effeminate man. Sometimes on our *RealFAMILIES* TV program, Dr. Jay Passavant and I get questions from mothers who are concerned over their sons sounding and acting effeminate. It is entirely appropriate for these mothers to tell their sons, "Listen, you're Mommy's *boy*; I don't like it when you act like a girl." They're teaching their sons how to be males and letting their sons know they value their identity as males. If your spouse's mother did this, you're reaping the rewards of a man who is secure in taking on the role of a husband.

It's possible for a mother to overdo this. In some situations, it's only natural for a boy to do "girlish" things. One of my early childhood memories is of playing paper dolls with my sister Sally. She was older than I was, so I invariably drifted into her world, and Sally certainly never asked me, "What do *you* want to do, Kevin?" Since she was older, I had to play on her terms if I wanted to play with her at all, and that meant playing with dolls. If your husband grew up with all sisters, he's probably very comfortable in the world of girls. There's a huge difference, however, in being comfortable *with* girls and always wanting to act *like* a girl.

Leman's Law #4:

Males who grow up to be mature adults have usually benefited from clearly defined gender roles. Confused kids rarely make consistently good life choices.

Males who grow up to be mature adults have usually benefited from clearly defined gender roles. I've never seen a confused kid make consistently good life choices. He'd better get his identity figured out before he gets married, or his wife will suffer accordingly.

Now let's consider the style of parenting your husband received. You may mistakenly assume that your father-in-law had the biggest influence on your husband. On the contrary, *your spouse's mother* probably had a greater impact on how your husband now treats you. You need to know: Was your husband's mom a "smother mother" or a "disciplining mother"?

A Smother Mother

Here's a terrifying truth that many mothers don't want to face: *A twelve-year-old son can do whatever he wants to do.* If he wants to smoke dope, he can. If he wants to steal cars, his mother can't stop him. If he's determined to kill somebody and is willing to die in the process, there is nothing a mother can do to prevent him.

I've seen mothers gape openmouthed, completely horrified when they realize that their once adorable three-year-old has suddenly grown up into a young man who is now wreaking havoc on the rest of the world. Listen to me: You can control a three-year-old, but you can't ultimately control a twelve-year-old. You can guide a child, but the opportunity to control a child at that age is extremely limited.

Your husband probably realized this before his mother did. He figured out that he could lie and get away with it, that he was smart enough to occasionally sneak out of the house, and that it was possible to hide the smell of cigarette smoke if he gave it some careful thought.

In this dawning of manhood, your husband's attitude toward women took a giant step forward into maturity, or it was frozen in a glacier of disrespect. Particularly because boys are so competitive, an overprotective mothering style is a prescription for disaster. Some moms won't let their children play sports because they don't want them to get hurt; they don't want them to climb trees because they might fall; they won't let them go on hikes because they might get lost; in short, they won't let them do the things that boys enjoy most. If you keep a boy from doing healthy things for eighteen years, he is going to completely rebel as soon as he gets the chance, and he won't rebel by doing healthy things—coaching his son's or daughter's basketball team or playing golf. Even worse, in many cases, the man won't be able to take it out on his mother, so he'll take it out on his wife.

Lucky you!

A smother mother often makes excuses for her boy. If the kid wants to duck out of school, she writes notes. If the boy runs off and plays before doing his chores, she shrugs her shoulders. If the boy wants to play Nintendo instead of doing his homework, she looks the other way.

Accepting excuses from a child makes the weak weaker. If you've ever wondered why your husband might assume you'll cover for his mistakes and lie, allow me to enlighten you. He learned this early on from his mother. You see, the smother mother is all too willing to "bend" the truth to "protect" her little boy's reputation. Let's say the kids are late to school because Johnny and Susie were fighting all morning. The smart mom will put that bit of information in the note! She won't let the kids even *think* she'd cover for them. Instead, she'll write, "Dear Teacher, Johnny is late for school because he was irresponsible this morning and kept fighting with his sister instead of getting ready." The smother mother, on the other hand, will come up with a lame excuse that preserves her son's "image" by sacrificing his long-term character.

> **Leman's Law #5:**
>
> Accepting excuses from a child makes the weak weaker.

My kids know that I will die for them, provide for them, protect them, forgive them, and love them, but *I will never lie for them.* I won't make them weaker by allowing them to avoid personal responsibility.

When a mother refuses to lie for her son, she teaches him that women aren't for using. I see a lot of men "hide" behind their wives. They use their wives to hide their drinking or their goofing off on the job, or they use their wives to cover for them with their parole officers. These "grown" men have learned that women cover up for men.

One of a mother's important jobs (or a schoolteacher's, or any woman who works with boys) is to teach boys to learn to *respect* women, not to use them. When a woman demands that her husband respect her, she's doing a great service for her son. Junior will see first-hand that a mom doesn't allow a dad to run over her. When he gets married, he'll assume that every husband should respect his wife.

If your husband's mom was a weak woman, your husband probably thinks all women are weak. If he learned early on that he could control and manipulate his mom, he'll assume that he can control and manipulate you. If you've married into this situation, you've got to take charge. Lovingly, but forcefully, you're going to have to stand up for yourself and show strength.

Keep in mind that there are degrees of smothering. Take a few moments to consider how your man was raised as a boy, particularly with respect to his view of women. On a scale of one to ten (one meaning that he has always used women, and ten meaning that he has the highest respect for women), where would you place your husband? It's unlikely that you can take a "one" and move him up to a "nine," but you can take a "six" and, with consistent effort, end up with an "eight." The principles we'll discuss later in this book will help you. For now, I want you to see that your husband will define you in relation to his mother, especially in regard to how she raised him.

Perfect Perry?

Another thing to consider is whether your husband's mom gave him room to fail. On *RealFAMILIES* I got a question from a woman who was clearly smothering her son. She practically followed Joey around the house, scolding, "Pick up your shoes! Keep your elbows off the table! Tuck in your shirt!"

I finally asked her, "How would you like it if someone followed you around the house with a pad and pencil, writing down all the things you did wrong? 'Clean that table again! Wash off the counter! Oops, you missed a piece of lint when you vacuumed the living room!'"

"I wouldn't like it at all," she said.

"Of course not, and neither does your son! We parents mess up and kids do too. Don't hold your son to a standard you can't match." In Christian language, I was asking this woman to temper her good intentions with grace. We need standards and principles, but I'm always suspicious of rules. When I think of guiding principles, I think of Jesus' approach to life. When I think of rules, I think of the Pharisees' approach to life.

Too many people in Christian homes mimic the Pharisees more than they imitate Jesus. I applaud parents who want to raise respectful and good-mannered kids, but berating them on an hourly basis is not the best way to achieve these traits.[2]

If your husband was never given the freedom to fail, he's going to react somewhat explosively to your corrections. You might think it's a minor thing to point out that the mirror he hung is a bit crooked, but he hears, "You've messed up! You're an absolute failure!" You don't mean to convey this impression, but because of his rearing, *that's what your husband hears*. In his mind, there are no degrees of success, only pass or fail.

You can rely on two ways to ask for improvement without setting off your husband's sensors of a performance-based self-worth. First, create a relationship of total acceptance and frequent affirmation—not just on what he does, but based on who your husband is. Brag about him in front of his face! Let him know that you appreciate the character qualities his mother might have missed, and that despite some of his shortcomings, you're delighted with your "catch." You'll need to be consistent and persistent because you're working to overcome a boyhood (eighteen years or more) of negative training. There's no overnight success for this exercise!

Second, add some sugar to corrections. For instance, you could say, "That looks terrific, Honey. You've put the mirror exactly where I want it. It's so good of you to get that done. I wonder, however, if it's a little crooked? Do you think that's a problem, or is it just me?"

Trust me—you can't compete with a mother's upbringing. You can only work around it. You married a man with a history, and you ignore that history at your peril.

If you're fortunate, you married a man with a disciplining mother rather than a smother mother.

A Disciplining Mother

The first mark of a disciplining mother is that *she doesn't do anything for her kids that they can do for themselves.* I'm not suggesting that a mother should refuse to serve her children a glass of milk when they ask for it. But have you ever gone to a science fair and realized that there were one or two projects that were actually done by the kids, not by their parents? Some parents are so concerned with creating the *impression* that their kids are the best that they teach their children to put image over substance and display something that the kids know they didn't build.

Here's where that type of training will lead: That same child will continue to place image over substance as he gets older. He'll be all promise and no performance at work. He'll look faithful to his wife but have a honey on the side. He'll give his mom the trappings of a son's devotion—a card or present for Mother's Day—but not the substance (you can bet his wife or secretary will buy that card).

Recognize this man? (Maybe *you've* purchased that card!)

If your husband's mother refused to participate in discipline, instead just handing it over to her husband, chances are that your spouse doesn't take you very seriously. A child must develop respect early on, and the wise mom will use the value of shock to get her point across. For example, if a son says something very hurtful—he says, "I hate you," or he swears at his mom—the disciplining mother won't fall apart. Instead, she'll maintain her composure, and when he comes to her later that day and reminds her that he needs a ride to his basketball game, she'll calmly say, "I'm sorry, Billy, but you're not going to the game."

Billy is mystified. "What do you mean, I'm not going to the game? We talked about it this morning!"

"That's right, we did," she'll answer. "But that was before you spoke disrespectfully to me, which I don't appreciate."

Waiting until just the right moment will create a shock value that will really open this boy's ears. Dressed, ready to go out the door, he'll never forget this lesson. If your husband's mom caved in, however, your husband probably treats your request as an irritation rather than something he should take seriously.

Much of what I've just described is about the wise *mother*. The wise *wife* will take all this into account, inventorying her husband's upbringing. Remember: You didn't marry a "clean slate." Your man was shaped, formed, and molded by another woman. She had him for eighteen years (at least), and she had the privilege of working with him when he was still developing.

One final inventory you need to take is the degree to which your man is driven.

Driven Men

Do you ever wonder why your husband can't slow down? Why he always has to keep moving, keep working, and even playing hard as if he was working?

Let me provide a clue. Once again, that's probably the way he was raised. His parents kept him busy, busy, busy. I find more and more men in my office who have no idea of what a socializing family is all about. Many of the men never enjoyed leisurely meals at home with their parents. Instead of taking vacations with their siblings, they were off by themselves at sports camps. The groom thus enters marriage with a radically different view of what a family is and does from the image that his bride cherishes.

Although this lifestyle is also true of many young women, parents naturally drive their sons a little harder and often keep them a little busier. Raising boys in this way can produce disastrous results.

Sports Illustrated ran a shocking cover story in its September 13, 1999, issue, asking "Who's coaching your kids?" The story detailed the long-running practice of several pedophiles who found coaching sports to be an ideal cover that gave them ready access to young boys.

The article revealed that many mothers unwittingly but gladly gave up their sons to these men. When a coach invites one child for a "sleep-over," parents ought to be suspicious. A young boy's participation in a team sport coached by an older man is one thing; a young boy's sharing a house with a much older, unmarried man is quite another.

Don't get me wrong. I respect coaches, 99 percent of whom are honorable men. My son-in-law is a coach! But some parents get so busy, they seem almost eager to pawn off their children to anyone willing to watch them, never slowing down long enough to ask themselves, *Why does this man show so much interest in my child?*

If your husband has been programmed to be driven, I've got to be honest with you: You're going to face a lifelong battle getting him to slow down. The best you can hope for is to do it by degrees.

You can avoid passing on this tendency to the next generation, however. One way to combat it is quite simple: Get your kids out of most activities. We had a guest at our house, an editor who was visiting from out of town. It was during December, so our son, Kevin, was home from college. Krissy and her husband, Dennis, came over too. After watching how close our kids were and how much they enjoyed being together, this editor asked me, "How do you raise a family like yours?"

"What do you mean?" I asked.

"How do you build a home where everybody wants to be together?"

"It's all about bonding," I replied. "The Lemans have never been big joiners. If our kids had traveled three different directions five or six nights a week, we'd never have had time to bond as a family. But since we severely limited outside activities, we spent and still spend lots of time together—which is why our family members want to be together today. We actually *like* each other."

The pace that some families set for themselves is crazy. I've talked to parents whose kids started tumbling and gymnastics when they were age three or four, soccer at age five, T-ball at age six, and karate lessons at age seven. I know of a ten-year-old boy—an only child—whose mom allowed him to play on three different basketball teams *during the same season!* That approach to bringing up children is nuts! Our seven-year-old Lauren isn't in *anything*. Some might call her deprived, but I wish you could see her face when big brother Kevin comes home. There's no place she'd rather be than by his side! The last time Kevin came home from college, Lauren got up in the middle of the night, pulled her blankets off her bed, and went into Kevin's room so that she could sleep on the floor, right next to him.

If your son's schedule includes Scouts on Monday, basketball practice on Tuesday and Thursday, band practice on Wednesday, and basketball games on Friday and Saturday (not to mention youth group on Sunday), when is he going to have a chance to bond with you or his siblings?

Our kids love each other because they've bonded together. They've bonded together because they've spent time together. It's a simple recipe. As your kids get older, you'll appreciate their relationship all the more. Few things in life are more fulfilling for me than to sit at my dinner table with my adult children and their spouses filling the seats, talking and laughing and thoroughly enjoying being together, while the younger children join in.

> **Leman's Law #6:**
> A family isn't something you're given;
> a family is something you create.

Creating a family takes more than a few hurried moments in bed, followed by nine months of waiting and a rather messy birth. That *begins* a family, but it doesn't *maintain* one. Creating a family takes spending time together, eating common meals, playing games together, and talking to each other. You can't do that if the house becomes a hotel.

The pace of our culture has gotten so busy that I can say to virtually any parent reading this book, "Whatever activities your child is in, cut them by half." You may choose to disagree, but if you do, don't be surprised that your children are less than excited about getting together again as soon as they are old enough to be out on their own.

This principle of protecting your boy by limiting his outside activities goes beyond bonding. If you really want to make a difference in your son's life, you must spend time with him. That's the *only* way. If you want your son to pick up how to relate to women from you rather than from sixteen-year-old Sally down the street, you have to ask yourself: *Am I willing to spend as much time with him as Sally is?*

Limiting all these activities takes a strong woman, but you've got to save your son from himself. He'll run himself ragged if you let him. He needs you to put on the brakes, redirect his energy, and keep him focused enough so that he can concentrate on the things in life that really matter.

The Biggest Imprint of All

Some more discerning readers may have wondered when I was going to touch on the most sensitive subject of all. The truth is, your husband's sexual appetite was whetted long before he kissed you in front of a church full of people and began sweating at the mere thought of your honeymoon. His hormones started heating up much earlier than you could ever imagine.

But this topic is big enough to warrant a chapter on its own. I'm about to introduce you to the world your husband has probably never had the guts to tell you about. The reality is that he has been thinking about sex for a long time—long before you came into the picture.

What Is It About Boys and Sex?

My friend Neil Clark Warren tells a funny and all-too-common story about when he was little. He was just three years old when his mother handed him a soaped-up washcloth and said, "Wash your thing."

Neil thought, *My thing? I know where my elbow is, I know where my knees are, and I've even found my armpit—but my thing?*

Neil's experience is not that unusual. Most mothers are somewhat uncomfortable with their boys' sexuality. The result is that your husband probably had to learn much of what he knows about sex on his own—with some very unfortunate consequences.

Joey's Real Best Friend

True story: a young mother was giving her three-year-old son a bath when he looked up and said, "Mommy, I love my penis."

The young mom became flustered, so she launched into an anatomy lesson. "Well, Honey, God made us, and He gave us elbows and fingers and toes and knees and ears and feet—and every part is just as important as every other part."

The boy didn't say a word, listening patiently to his mom's lesson on the wonders of the human body. When she finished, he said, "But, Mommy, I still like my penis the best."

As a boy hits eight and nine years old, he starts to think a lot about sex but probably isn't talking about it much. All of that will change dramatically, usually around the age of eleven, twelve, or thirteen.

Here's what was *really* going on in your husband's mind when he was a little boy. For starters, most boys are fascinated with their penises, and why shouldn't they be? The penis has the potential to bring the most exquisite pleasure as well as (if it is hit) the most extreme pain. Regular bodily processes require the boy to hold the penis several times a day. It's always there, a little companion that every boy meets, stares at—and usually plays with—several times a day.

But that penis also represents a virtual sexual time bomb that goes off between the ages of ten and fifteen. From that point, your husband became a *very* sexual being. As a female, you were probably drawn emotionally to boys at this age, but your husband wasn't mesmerized by thoughts of long walks in the park. On the contrary, he was fascinated with the mere glimpse of a bra strap or the most innocuous panty lines protruding from a girl's gym shorts.

Your husband's time bomb was ignited with his first nocturnal emission. These nocturnal emissions are almost always accompanied by a *very* sexual dream. That's right—even when your husband was just a boy, he began having virtually involuntary sexual fantasies! That was true regardless of his morality. I was never caught up in pornography as a young man, but even without the outside stimulation, my first dream was so explicit that I can *still* remember it (sometimes, I wish it would come back for a rerun!). It is normal for a young boy at this age to dream about having sex, with either a girl his age or an older woman. Your husband had little control over the dreams and shouldn't have felt any shame over them, but most boys raised in Christian homes do (often because their moms can't imagine how thinking about sex at this age could possibly be innocent; therefore, they make their sons feel guilty for demonstrating any interest at all).

> **Leman's Law #7:**
> Your husband's sexual awakening had nothing to do with his morality; it had everything to do with his hormones. A boy's morality will govern what he thinks about and how he behaves, but it won't keep sex from being a major influence in his life.

A mom who has never been privy to an excess of testosterone can have a particularly difficult time understanding how sexual her son can be. Even though you weren't around at that point in your husband's sexual development, his attitude toward you—his wife—was being profoundly shaped. You see, the only "woman" in his life at that time might have been someone who was either fearful or angry at his growing sexuality. Your husband's mother might have made him feel ashamed, and as a consequence, your husband might have learned to hide his sexuality from his mom, just as your husband might very well be hiding the depth and frequency of his sexual interest today because he has similar fears—that you will ridicule or shame him for being so sexual. He thinks, *That's just the way women are*.

At some point during this stage, your husband began masturbating. We psychologists like to point out that studies definitively show that 96 percent of boys masturbate[1]—and the other 4 percent are lying! This act is not something shameful; it's a natural part of growing up. In my experience dealing with clients, as well as my reading of various studies, it seems that the average boy will masturbate every other day. Sometimes this may become more frequent for a variety of reasons. Without a hang-up, however, the boy will eventually return to masturbating about fourteen or fifteen times a month.

You probably had no idea it was that frequent, did you?

Two things will increase this number. The first is a mother who attaches religious shame to the practice. In such households, the boy may become obsessed with *not* doing it, but he thinks about it all the more, of course. He will likely experience numerous sexual frustrations during marriage—most often, premature ejaculation. If your husband struggles with this (and more than 30 percent of men occasionally do), you know how frustrating this problem can be in the marriage bed.

The second is an overly sexualized home—with pornography running rampant and immodest, immoral parents modeling inappropriate behavior. This home can also result in excessive masturbation. If your husband grew up in this environment, he likely began viewing women as playthings that bring pleasure rather than as people who need to be served, honored, cherished, and respected.

Once again, we come back to balance. I believe we need to teach young boys the value of self-control without making them feel guilty for something that is virtually inevitable. There is a difference between telling a boy it's improper to drive his car 80 miles per hour and telling him never to drive faster than 25 miles per hour. The former is a safe, reasonable restraint; the latter is just plain unrealistic.

A very distraught young woman called me. I knew that she had grown up in a very conservative Christian home and that she and her fiancé were seriously considering serving on the mission field. During a late-night talk, her would-be husband confessed that he had struggled with masturbation for years. The young woman called me in great distress, thinking that the man she had fallen in love with was a closet pervert! She had no idea what boys can do.

As gently as possible, I tried to inform her that if she was waiting to find a man who had never masturbated, she had better plan on staying single for a *long* time—probably forever!

A Long Process

One of the biggest jokes in modern education is the concept of sex education in the schools. I'm not suggesting that sex education is necessarily inappropriate in this context (I've spoken on this topic at several schools). I am suggesting that the idea of providing sex education in a one-, two-, or three-week course is ludicrous.

Healthy sex education needs to be an *ongoing event*. It is not a talk or a series of talks. It is an ongoing dialogue that begins early in life about the differences between men and women—and about life in general. The likelihood of your husband having experienced sex education in this format, however, is not very high. Nor did he probably get it from the best teacher.

Let's consider this issue practically. Who is the ideal person to talk to a boy about sex? Most people will immediately say, "His father." Well, I'm not most people, so I have a different perspective. I vote that it should be his *mom*.

In my book *What a Difference a Daddy Makes*, I surprised many dads by suggesting that fathers should be the primary sex educators of their daughters. Who better knows what a man needs than another man? In the same way, who better can explain a woman's perspective on sexuality than a boy's mom? Look, little Joey already understands what it feels like to have a penis! What he doesn't know, but really wants to know, is how it feels to have two breasts, how girls react to boys, and how he can relate to the opposite sex without making a total fool of himself.

The key in terms of sex education is for the mother to take the lead and the father to become a part of it. The mom can pretend that nocturnal emissions don't exist, but that's not the healthiest position to take. It is much healthier for the boy if he can see his mom comfortably talk about how God created us as sexual beings.

I'm not suggesting that such talks are comfortable. They aren't any easier for me than they are for anybody else. I've seen the shock register on each daughter's face when she finally realized what her dad does with her mom. I remember eight-year-old Hannah asking me, "You really do that, Dad?"

"Just five times, Honey, only five times." (I have five kids.)

But if a woman can become more comfortable discussing these issues with her son, she can give him an unusually healthy and secure start in life. She can inaugurate little Joey into the world of turnoffs and turn-ons by telling him, "You might think it's funny to grab a girl's breast at school, but I'm telling you it hurts and it's a cruel thing to do. It's not something a girl enjoys." While this seems obvious to most females, keep in mind that 90 percent of the boys in Joey's junior high would *love* it if a girl came up behind them and grabbed their penises!

If I were a betting man, I could make a lot of money wagering that your husband didn't receive this kind of training. On the contrary, your husband and his mother probably pretended that the word *masturbation* didn't exist.

When shame, guilt, and condemnation are attached to this act, the boy will learn to hide his sexuality. He'll learn that women think his sex drive is shameful, horrible, and evil. Now, if a boy learns that, how do you think he'll learn to enjoy healthy and holy sexuality in marriage? Attaching shame and guilt to sex is likely to create an immature man who pleasures himself with pornographic magazines and who frequents strip clubs. He won't be able to enjoy sex unless it feels dirty and illicit.

Perhaps you are dealing with this situation. I've been describing your husband and his mother as if they were standing in front of me.

"Well, Dr. Leman," you might say, "if that's the case, what can I do about it?"

We're going to talk a great deal about sexuality within marriage in later chapters, so here let me offer a valuable two-word prescription: *Stop pretending.* Your husband has been extremely interested and at times obsessed with sex since he was a small boy. *Nothing has changed.* Will you be open with your husband about this, or will you continue to play the pretend game he played with his mother?

A great hurdle that your husband has had to overcome is the downward drift of the age of puberty. The age of puberty in this country is now lower than it has ever been in history, and it continues to drop. This may be due to good hygiene, improved health and nutrition, or normal human development, but little Joey is becoming a sexualized being much faster than boys did in his grandparents' generation. Your husband's mother didn't understand his burgeoning sexuality, and your husband's father might have been caught off guard too.

This early development had a major impact on your husband's sexual development, one that his great-great-grandfather didn't have to address. We need to face up to the difficulties created by the gap between the age of puberty and the age at which a young man marries.[2]

Not that long ago the amount of time between puberty and marriage was very small. Many boys didn't reach puberty until seventeen or eighteen, and they often married a year or two later. But the modern world has created a dangerous gap of ten or fifteen years. At the same time that the age of puberty has dropped to between twelve and fifteen, the average age at which a young man marries has risen to the mid- and upper twenties—providing a Grand Canyon–like gap of a decade or more. To be financially solvent, with a good job and his college education behind him, a young man might be close to thirty before he thinks he is economically ready for the responsibilities of starting a family, even though sexually he has been awakened for fifteen years.

Consequently, you've married a man with a long sexual history—even if he was a virgin. He has struggled with his sexuality from the time he was a boy. He has walked through the valley of shame, obsession, delight, ecstasy, and confusion, and then you came on the scene!

You may be delighted that your husband grew up in a "nice Christian home," but don't fool yourself into thinking that means everything was okay. Dr. Archibald Hart, a Christian psychologist and author, warns:

> Many, many fine moral and good men are haunted by feelings of lust, obsessions about sex, and compulsions to masturbate. This began with extreme feelings of guilt and shame generated during their teenage years . . . . Their obsessions and compulsions never subside, even after years of happy and sexually satisfying marriage. Only hard, dedicated work can remove them. The challenge before us is how to teach sexual self-control without creating neurotic guilt.[3]

An unfortunate consequence of this gap is an increasing use of pornography. Your husband probably has a history here too.

Boys and Pornography

My main theme throughout this chapter has been consistent: A boy becomes a very sexual being at an increasingly early age, but his mom may be either ashamed or afraid of this reality and remain silent, leaving the boy (who has grown up to be your husband) to fend for himself.

When boys are left to themselves, they tend to make poor choices (ever read *Lord of the Flies?*). Instead of having a loving, instructional talk with their parents about how to control their sexual urges, they trade back issues of *Playboy* and swap dirty stories. Boys seek to satisfy their curiosity, one way or another.

That is precisely why I strongly urge parents to get involved in their children's sexual development. Expecting a boy never to masturbate is unrealistic. Expecting a boy to masturbate without using pornographic materials or engaging in inappropriate fantasies is entirely reasonable. The trick is for parents to learn how not to turn young boys off with unreasonable prohibitions so that they can still influence them with disciplined guidance.

> **Leman's Law #8:**
>
> Sexually well-adjusted husbands usually had moms who learned that they couldn't erase their sons' sex drive, but that they could help their sons learn how to govern it.

A boy who learns how to govern his sexual urges grows up to be a man who is able to engage in healthy sexual relations.

One perhaps well-meaning but terribly destructive mother thought she had found a clever way to deal with her son's stash of pornography.

Mom found the nudie pictures in a box hidden underneath her son's bed. With a rush of indignation, she taped the pictures all over the living room, intentionally shaming her boy for bringing "that stuff" into her house. When the boy came into the house and saw the pictures, he just about fell over with feelings of shame and self-loathing, but the mother crowed, "That ended his career as an art collector!"[4]

Mom wrote to Ann Landers, proud of her clever parenting, and Ann concurred with what she had done, saying she thought the mom's response was "ingenious" and "amusing." In fact, it was just about the cruelest thing this mother could have done to a young boy traveling through a normal stage of life and trying to find his way. When she taped the pictures in the living room, she erected a twelve-foot-high wall between herself and her son. I bet that was the *last* conversation she ever had with her son about sex. She might have talked *at* him after that, but I guarantee you, she never got another chance to talk *with* him.

It's not that I'm soft on pornography. I've never been a user of pornography, even as a boy, and I believe from clinical evidence that the negative effects of pornography can be very severe. The problem is that few homes in this country are absolutely free of some type of pornographic exposure, and most boys will do all they can to satisfy their sexual curiosity accordingly.

If your husband has a porn stash lying around the house, it's only a matter of time until Junior and his friends start borrowing it. Wherever it is, they'll find it! "But my husband is a Christian!" you say. "He'd never leave that type of garbage lying around." Good for you—but are all the fathers of all your son's friends Christians who would "never leave that type of garbage lying around"? Little boys might trade cards with pictures of Ken Griffey Jr. on them; adolescent boys are notorious for trading pictures of Miss January.

Even in Christian homes, boys get creative. Do you subscribe to

National Geographic? For years, curious boys have feigned a sudden interest in foreign cultures, but their real aim is to catch a fleeting glimpse of a foreign body. To a sexually awakened young boy, a breast is a breast, whether that breast is displayed in an African desert or in Hugh Hefner's bedroom.

Advertisements are also boys' favorites. Even the Sears catalog uses real-life models of women wearing lingerie and bras. I know, I know: the bras cover up more than many swimsuits. But to a young boy's mind, they are still bras, and he can get terribly excited looking at them.

I've heard of young boys who wait in front of a scrambled cable channel, hoping that a momentarily interrupted scramble will provide the briefest glimpse of a bare breast or bottom. (This very act was recently immortalized in the hit—but very offensive—movie *American Pie.*)

The reason I'm telling you all this is to take away some of the shock when I mention that your husband has probably seen dozens—if not hundreds or even thousands—of naked or partially unclothed women. That's the sad fact of living in today's world. That's why you often rightly feel demeaned when your worth is tied to your physical appearance. It's impossible to compete—and you shouldn't be made to feel as if you need to. But in all likelihood, this exposure happened long before you met the man of your dreams.

The best thing you can do about this—if you truly want to understand your man—is to talk to your husband about his sexual past. Let him know that you know he has one, even if he was a virgin when you got married. Find out where that past was covered in shame and where he learned to hide. Although he had this sexual experience as a boy, it's not too late for him to face it as a man. He can go back and discard false notions of shame and guilt and embrace a more healthy view of sexuality.

When I say this, I don't mean to suggest that you and your husband should talk about every sexual incident that has ever occurred in your husband's life. *I'm a firm believer that many details—especially in this arena—are better left unsaid.* Some things you don't want to know about and *shouldn't* know about. When I suggest talking with your husband about his sexual past, I mean talking with him about how he developed sexually—in general terms. Was his mom supportive? Was the subject completely ignored? Where did his education come from, and how is that affecting him today?

Husbands and wives hide from these issues every bit as much as mothers and sons do. I want this book to open your eyes, and this may be the biggest eye-opener of them all: for the vast majority of his life, your husband has been a *very* sexual being.

I've painted a picture of your husband as a young man. In the next part we'll discuss what made him seem so attractive to you. Have you ever considered *why* you married the man you married? Well, you're going to find out!

PART 2

The Man Who Matters Most

4

Why You Married the Man You Married

Have you ever awakened late at night and asked yourself *why* you married the man you married? I know, I know: you fell in love. But *why* did you fall in love with *this particular guy?* What was it about him that got your heart beating a little faster—besides his fabulous teeth or warm smile? What made you think that out of all the billions of men living on the planet, he was the one you'd most like to share your life with?

It's a healthy exercise to figure this out, and the answer isn't nearly as mysterious as you might think. I'm going to let you in on a little secret: Fathers leave an indelible imprint on their little girls. Whether you're reacting out of love or hate, you're probably reacting to your father's influence. Whenever I'm trying to figure out why any woman chose any man, I begin with the woman's dad (even the absence of a dad will affect the man you choose).

All of us are, in part, products of our environment. Either we are reaping the benefits of having good parents, or we have been placed at risk as the result of poor parenting. Marriage amplifies this phenomenon. You are quite literally paying for the sins (or reaping the rewards) of your mother-in-law. Conversely, your husband is paying for the sins (or reaping the rewards) of your father.

Added to this is the influence of your brothers and sisters (or lack thereof), including your birth order in the family. I discuss family-of-origin issues at length in *The New Birth Order Book* (which I recommend that you read to understand this concept more fully), so I won't go into detail here. But you need to understand that your childhood family has radically affected the person you have become and the man you choose (or have chosen) to marry.

To help you understand why you married the man you married, I'd like to walk you through three real conversations that I've had with women. Each woman graciously agreed to have her interview taped and then transcribed so you could see for yourself the process I typically go through in helping a woman understand why she married the man she married.

As you read, ask yourself the same questions that I ask them. The exercise will be invaluable as you seek to understand what first drew you to your husband so that you can learn how to work toward an even better relationship today.

Judging Amy

Amy was twenty-three years old when she married Mike, and they had been married about a year and a half by the time I talked to her. The first question I asked her was, "How would you describe yourself as a little kid between the ages of five and ten?"

"I was strong-willed, always liked to be the boss. I was certainly the leader with my friends."

"Let me guess," I said. "You were the oldest child."

"That's right!"

"Tell me some more."

"I had a very strong conscience and liked to try new things. I was a terrible liar and would always confess when I did something wrong. I loved going to church with my mom, but I didn't like school. I talked a lot in class."

"You were sort of the social lion, weren't you?"

"Yes, I was."

The first thing I always want to find out when dissecting a woman's marital choice is how she describes herself as a child. (When you describe yourself as a child, you're usually able to be more objective than if you were to describe yourself as an adult. For some reason, it seems less personal. You think, *That's who I was* then. But do you know what? It's also usually a pretty good picture of who you are *now*. You may be more moral and disciplined, but you probably carry the same traits.)

If you really want to understand why you married the man you married, you need to accept Leman's Law # 9.

> **Leman's Law #9:**
>
> The little girl you once were, you still are.

You'll never migrate very far from that little girl.

Next, I ask the woman to describe one of her parents. Though I don't say this ahead of time, I'm not listening only for the description; I'm equally interested in *which* parent she chooses to describe. Whichever one she chooses is the one who probably influenced her most.

Amy chose her mom.

"My mom is very social but different from me," she said. "Everybody that meets her likes her. She's a chatterbox, the kind that will tell a clerk or a stranger all about her family. She's somewhat submissive because she likes to please others, but she's very disciplined. She gets up early every morning. She eats right and exercises consistently."

I now ask for an early childhood recollection. Lastborns usually say something happy. I know a lastborn woman whose dad took her out for lunch just one time in her life, but that memory comes first to her mind. Since Amy is a firstborn, I expected something much different, and I was not disappointed.

"Well, I'm somewhat embarrassed to say this," she said, "but . . ."

"Let me guess," I broke in, "and make this a little easier for you. You violated a rule, didn't you?"

"That's right. I got in a car with a stranger to get a ride to school when I was five years old."

At that point I had a pretty tidy portrait of Amy: as a firstborn, she's a strong-willed, bossy little sucker who has a strong conscience, and who is very much a black-and-white thinker.

For the purpose of this book, I edited some of her comments, but if you listened to the entire tape, you'd hear her using the word *very* a lot. Her mother was *very* disciplined, *very* social, *very* talkative.

I suggested—and Amy concurred—that Amy had a lot of perfectionism in her life. I tried to help Amy by introducing her to her "rule book," her unstated assumptions about how life is supposed to be lived. Though wives rarely share their rule books with their husbands—and may not know they have them—the rule books are behind 90 percent of marital disagreements. The husband unintentionally violates a rule he didn't know existed, and the wife thinks, *Why did he react that way?* or *Why did he say that?*

Some rule books suggest that conflicts are to be avoided at all costs. If a woman marries a man who expects that relationships involve heated debates, even yelling, they'll have a difficult time learning to relate to each other. Few young couples are mature enough to evaluate these many unstated assumptions. Each partner assumes that everyone else handles conflict the way the childhood family did.

"What did you expect marriage to be like, Amy?"

"I expected it to be like my parents' marriage. They're best friends and have a deep companionship. This 'togetherness' was my most important anticipation. I really had no negative worries. When I walked down the aisle, I just hoped my marriage would turn out to be just like my parents'."

This information was helpful, but I knew no marriage can live up to idealistic standards, so I asked, "When I say expectation minus reality equals disillusionment, does that mean anything to you?"

"Yeah," Amy said. "I had an unspoken expectation that my husband would be like my dad. My dad was a handyman, and I knew I was marrying an intellectual, but I still assumed Mike could fix our car when it broke down."

We were getting into her rule book. I asked Amy to describe her dad.

"Growing up, I always thought he had no emotions. I never saw him cry. He was really a black-and-white person who still loved us deeply—I never questioned his commitment, but he didn't hug me." She paused. "I think he hugged me once at my wedding."

"Who impacted your life more—your mom or your dad?"

"I adore my dad more than my mom, but if I had a problem, I'd call my mom. My dad is the distant hero."

"Who do you think impacted your life more when it came to marrying Mike?"

"My dad."

"I think you're right, so give me more descriptions of your dad."

"My dad was funny, the life of the party, but all my friends were afraid of him. He was intimidating because he was strong, a little rough, a police officer turned detective."

"Was he the firstborn or an only child?" I asked.

"No, but his sisters were a lot older, so it was like he was an only child. How did you know that?"

"Because cops are firstborns or only borns in overwhelming numbers. Notice you had an easier time describing your mom than your dad. You may be emotionally closer to your mom, but the model of who you married is wrapped up in your dad."

It was time to migrate over to Mike, Amy's husband.

"Give me a description of Mike."

"He's very laid-back, funny, very strong, *very* strong, both physically and in his opinions. He's creative and *very* social. He can have a conversation with anyone. He's very playful, but not emotional. I've never seen him cry, but he tells me he has cried before, like when his dad died [Mike was eight years old at the time]."

Notice this. Amy grew up with an intimidating, emotionally distant dad, the superhero type. And she married a man who is strong and always in control, and whom she has never seen cry. Are you catching the pattern?

Amy admitted to being a little "afraid" of Mike when they first met, but that didn't scare her off because she was comfortable with strong men. She loved the way Mike challenged her intellectually, debating theology long into the night. She said she knew she wanted to marry Mike just three months after they started spending time together, but they dated another two years before they married.

Though Mike is strong, he is also very "laid-back," which has been almost forced on him by his upbringing. After his dad died, he pretty much had to make it on his own as the oldest child in a somewhat chaotic family. Because his house was not well structured or neat, he had to adapt to tension and uncertainty without getting stressed out.

Amy relishes this calm. She wants to feel secure and safe. Her dad made her feel very safe—he wore a badge, after all, and intimidated all her friends—so Mike is a pretty good fit for her.

Our differences, however, give us what I call "couple power," the quality that produces satisfying marriages. You're in a great place when you need your spouse, and Amy says she needs Mike to help her take a more laid-back approach to life. Mike needs Amy to initiate. It's not so surprising that Amy initiates sex more than Mike does.

Before Mike, Amy considered dating another guy but decided that he was "too great." By that she meant too *compliant*, too agreeable. Though acting this way may be polite, it isn't attractive, at least not to a woman like Amy. "I'm not attracted to people who always give in to me," she said, "and I knew I could win every battle with that other guy. I didn't want just an equal. I wanted someone stronger because that's what a man is to me."

Powerful people respect power in other people. As a firstborn woman, Amy needs a powerful man. Her image of masculinity was shaped by a dad who wore a badge; you can't get much stronger than that in the eyes of a little girl.

Amy's dad influenced her choice of Mike, yet who she is today is probably tied up in her mom. Amy told me, "Sometimes I pray to the Lord and ask Him, 'Why did You give me this personality *and* make me a woman?'"

I had a good answer: "So you can stay married to Mike."

Mike is a good fit for Amy. It's very important for Amy that Mike is physically and emotionally strong, and it's an added bonus that he fulfills an emotional need she didn't get as a little kid—words of affirmation and physical affection. Some of Amy's friends worried about her relationship with Mike because they saw the couple bicker a lot, but Amy enjoys going "head to head." It leads to more respect, not less, and Mike's laid-back style makes it even better.

Julie—Finding the Key

Julie and Peter have been married for fifteen years. I began our interview by asking her, "What first attracted you to Peter?"

She didn't hesitate before saying, "His friendship with other males; he had a lot of good, close guy friends." Julie added that she appreciated Peter's sense of humor and his leadership, but she was so strong with the first point that I immediately guessed Julie grew up with mostly sisters.

She did. She's the lastborn in a family with six children, but her older brother is twelve years older than she is, so she never really remembers living with him (he's so distant in her life that he once confused Julie and her sister at the airport). Added to this, Julie's father grew up without sisters. He felt somewhat uncomfortable around females, particularly what he perceived to be Julie's "hypersensitivity." As the "baby girl" in the family, Julie more than likely expected to be treated with special deference, and her father, who already had a difficult time relating to girls, no doubt felt over his head trying to parent an extremely sensitive girl.

Julie said her relationship with her father "wasn't close. I don't have any negative feelings, except he got frustrated with my sensitivity."

She was also shy—a trait that is unusual in a lastborn, but understandable, given Julie's family of origin. Her next older sister was the rebellious one, which means that Julie reacted by being very compliant and scared.

I asked Julie to describe Peter's family background. Peter was the third of four children, but his two older brothers were seven and ten years older than he was. He spent most of his time with his younger sister and thus assumed some characteristics of a firstborn. (Any gap of more than five years between children is significant.) His neighborhood was filled with girls, and there were two women in the neighborhood whom Peter described as "second moms." Though Peter played a lot of sports with older boys, he was extremely comfortable relating to females of all ages.

Men and boys intimidated Julie. She had few male friends and lacked a close brother, so she was never comfortable around boys. Peter's level of comfort with females was a huge draw for her. Through Peter—who, you'll recall, had many close male friends—Julie could finally get to know the other gender.

But Julie's lack of familiarity with males showed during their honeymoon. While she and Peter were dating, she became aware that Peter was "very physically oriented, very huggy," and on the honeymoon she realized that "hugginess" had turned into something else entirely.

"The reality hit me that his need and desire for sex and my difference in that area were going to be an issue."

Julie described her marriage to Peter as "very close," and their friends agreed. It took Julie almost ten years, however, to come to grips with Peter's sexual hunger. "I love to cook and he loves to eat, so I tried to serve him with nice meals. But I eventually found out that that wasn't good enough without a lot of good sex."

She has an understanding of this point that goes far beyond that of younger wives.

"Julie," I said, "how many times a day do you think Peter has a sexual thought?"

She laughed. "He says about every two minutes or some ridiculous amount. With him it might be twenty times!"

"And if I asked him how many times you have a sexual thought, what would he say?"

"He'd say maybe one if he's lucky."

Though they differ greatly in this area, it was refreshing to hear how well they understand each other. Julie is under no illusion about how Peter likes to be loved. His favorite birthday present, she said, would be for her to visit Victoria's Secret and bring home something new for him to see on her—and I'm sure she's correct.

"Have you figured out the similarities between your husband and father?"

Julie hesitated. "Peter denies it, but I think he is a bit of a controller, though he works at that. He doesn't like being a controller, but he's definitely a 'fixer.' My dad's the same way. The difference is, Peter works at getting better. He wants me to make decisions independent of him."

I should mention that Peter is a senior vice president at his company. He must have leadership skills and a "fix it" mentality to succeed at his job, and again, it's a positive sign that he's working not to bring that same mentality home with him—though it's only natural that control will be somewhat of an issue for him.

Julie is pretty easy to map: she didn't have practical experience with males or a particularly close relationship with her dad. Peter, who had tons of close male friends and who was very comfortable around women—making it unusually easy for Julie to talk to him—stood out like a sore thumb (in a good way). He was everything she needed.

But because Julie wasn't familiar with men, Peter's sex drive was an absolute mystery for almost a decade. She could compare Peter only to her sisters and herself, and Peter's libido didn't come close to matching up there. What she found so attractive about Peter—that he was a guy she could relate to and through whom she could relate to other guys—also had the negative of not preparing her for how *different* guys can be. You don't get one without the other.

Fortunately, Peter and Julie have come out on the other side and now have a much more mature understanding. About seven years into their marriage, they went away for a weekend without the kids, and each one made a promise to the other. Peter said, "I'll promise to think about how to be more romantic if you'll promise to think more about sex."

To her credit, Julie thought it was a fair deal. Since sex was so important to Peter, she realized she needed to consciously think about sex more if she really loved him. She will never think about sex as much as Peter does, but she can at least boost her "once a day" to three to five times.

I think they're on their way to having a great and lasting marriage.

Marcy—Defying the Odds

Marcy is twenty-four years old and has been married for two and a half years. Her self-described personality as a little kid was "rambunctious, cheerful, giggly, and affectionate." She was the younger of two daughters for most of her life. Her parents divorced when she was five, and her mom remarried several years later, parenting two young children. The older child of the second marrage is ten years younger than Marcy, which means that Marcy has taken on the character of a lastborn.

When I asked Marcy to describe one of her parents, I wasn't surprised when she chose her mom, calling her "hospitable, compassionate, selfless, funny, and humorous."

I asked her, "Is your mom who you try to be?"

Marcy immediately said, "Oh yeah, definitely."

She described her biological father as "a workaholic, selfish, and lacking commitment." She met her stepdad, whom she calls her "real dad," when she was seven years old. She felt "very close" to him as she was growing up, though she admitted tension arose as she reached adolescence.

Matt, her husband, is a mail carrier, about six years older than Marcy. She spoke of him as "very sincere, very honest, loyal, supportive, encouraging, very faithful, smart." Matt is a third born in a family with four children. Middle children tend to be people pleasers, so I wasn't caught off guard when Marcy said she was first attracted to Matt's kindness.

Let me break in here and say it is extremely unusual for a woman in Marcy's situation—not having a healthy father relationship until she was almost a preteen—to marry a guy who sounds as fabulous as Matt. Women with similar backgrounds usually migrate to the losers, the jerks, and the woman haters. The deck is definitely stacked against someone like Marcy, but something happened in her life to prevent marital disaster. Further adding to my surprise, Marcy's older sister married well.

I asked Marcy why she thought she and her sister had chosen such good husbands. She answered, "From my mom's and my biological dad's relationship I learned what I *didn't* want."

That wasn't good enough for me. Plenty of women promise themselves that, but then turn around and marry guys like their moms married.

Still looking for the reason why Marcy avoided the trap too many women fall into, I began to focus on her mom, who I thought must be an absolutely incredible woman.

"She is," Marcy confirmed. "She's wonderful."

Another positive element was that her mom married a dedicated Christian and pastor who modeled a relationship of commitment, forgiveness, and sensitivity. Marcy watched her mom remarry "for the right reasons." Though it came relatively late in life, Marcy and her sister had an opportunity to see a good marriage.

Marcy understands her husband's need to be respected and admired, and she realizes that Matt isn't going to fulfill all the roles of a husband she originally expected—such as "being in charge of the finances and doing mechanical things; he's not that great at those"—but she's okay with that.

Their division of labor is pretty good. Matt helps out a lot around the house and does virtually all the yard work. For having been married less than three years, they are doing surprisingly well, though I suspect Marcy may not fully understand the extent of her husband's sexual needs. When I asked her to list Matt's primary needs, she listed four things—affirmation, respect, support, and love—without mentioning sexual fulfillment. I asked her how many times she thought Matt had had a sexual thought that day.

She guessed two.

Ahem. If Matt is like most men, he had several sexual thoughts before he left the house for work. But understanding all this takes time. Many couples are married for ten years or more before these more "sensitive" areas of their needs and desires are fully known to each other.

Marcy is truly one of the 10 percent, the very few who escape from such a poor start. She admitted that she had feelings of abandonment by her biological dad, but that she was able to deal with them "through Jesus." And now she feels very secure in her husband's love and commitment. Ninety percent of the women in Marcy's situation would describe their greatest fear as abandonment by their husbands, but not Marcy. Though that was true early in her relationship with Matt, it is true no longer. Again, I suspect the success of her mom's second marriage is helping her.

The parent you describe first is always the most influential, so Marcy described her mom. I've never met this woman, but she must be an amazing character to steer two daughters through such choppy waters and have them marry so well.

Notice what attracted Marcy to Matt: his kindness, faithfulness, and loyalty. She didn't learn that this is how a man relates to his wife by watching her biological father; she must have learned it from her step-dad. And having witnessed her mother's heartache from being married to an unfaithful man, she knew with an iron will what she wanted to avoid. She treasures a committed man, and she has found one in Matt.

Is Family of Origin Your Destiny?

Marcy is proof that a woman can grow up with a poor parental role model and still enjoy a successful marriage, but remember, *women who have had a difficult start in life due to a poor parental role model need to watch themselves.* I can tell you your temptation right now: you're going to want to become a "Martha Luther" and try to reform an unreformable man. Or you may try to be a "Donna Quixote," losing yourself in an idealistic mission of marriage that will ultimately destroy you. Your life is so hard that you think it can't possibly get any worse, and you think that this man, flawed as he is, might actually make it a little better, so you take a few shortcuts, get married without really knowing him, and pay dearly and long for your lack of caution.

If you come from a troubled background, remind yourself constantly that you are probably going to be drawn to men who will not be good for you. If you were not affirmed as a daughter—if your femininity was challenged rather than encouraged—you'll actually feel more comfortable with a man who treats you like a doormat than you will with a man who respects you.

You see how much your father has affected you, so let's spend a few chapters looking a little more carefully at this father-daughter relationship.

Coming to Grips with Father Hunger

"Daddy, are you going to be home by 6:30 on Tuesday?"

"No, Lauren, I won't. My plane doesn't land until 9:30."

"But, Daddy, you'll miss my two songs! I'm going to sing in the play!"

I could hear the panic in Lauren's voice, and when Sande got on the phone, she confirmed that Lauren was crying.

That's all I needed to hear. I canceled an afternoon talk show (leaving behind a panicked producer), pleaded my case with American Airlines, and got an early morning flight back to Tucson.

As Lauren and her mother pulled up at the airport, Lauren was expecting to see her brother, Kevin, who was returning from college that same day. When she saw me, her face lit up the terminal.

The first thing I said was, "Daddy is going to be able to hear you sing tonight."

Lauren ran up and hugged me, yelling out, "My daddy, my daddy, my daddy! Oh, goody, goody, goody!"

We got to the play, and I couldn't wait until Lauren had a chance to sing. Imagine my surprise when she was surrounded by twenty-eight other kids.

"Uh, Honey?" I asked Sande. "I thought Lauren was going to sing two songs."

"She is," Sande answered.

"Well, maybe I'm crazy, but the way Lauren reacted, I assumed she was singing two *solos.*"

"No, she's singing in a group."

"You mean, I canceled a talk show and flew home to hear Lauren sing *in a group?*"

"It doesn't matter whether you can actually hear her," Sande said. "What matters is that you're here. That's what she'll remember."

You know what? There's a bit of Lauren in every little girl—a father hunger that can't be stilled. Most people realize that, but many women don't realize that there's a bit of Lauren in every grown woman—a father hunger that still won't go away, even after you've left home.

I'm warning you in advance: this next section is going to be very difficult for some readers. Many readers have been blessed with wonderful, loving fathers. If that's you, a lot of what I'm about to say might not make much sense. Others of you have had terrible fathers, but you haven't wanted to admit it. I need to address this latter group now, helping you to "give up the ghost" so you can gain a more accurate understanding of the man who has profoundly marked your life. Until you understand the true extent of the damage done by Daddy Attention Deficit Disorder (DADD), you'll never be free to pursue unhindered other healthy relationships with men.

Fantasy Fathers

Despite having been abused, a woman may continue to view her father as a benevolent protector and ally, even though he treated her like an enemy. I've seen this happen too many times. Imagine a typical jerk husband/father. He cheats on his wife. He neglects his daughter. Out of ten birthdays, he's home for one. He couldn't tell you the name of his daughter's school. You ask him for the name of his child's pediatrician, and all you'll get in response is a blank stare. He doesn't have a clue about what his daughter really likes. He may buy her a ridiculously young toy for her age, having been so preoccupied he didn't notice that she has graduated from playing with Barbies to singing along with CDs.

Got him in your mind?

Now verbally attack that man in front of his daughter, and watch her defend him with all the vehemence of a presidential candidate.

What's going on?

> **Leman's Law #10:**
>
> The need for a strong father figure is so great that a woman may invent a father who never was and then tack that invention onto her real father, entering an elaborate game of make-believe.

There are degrees of this invention. To keep the glittering image alive, the daughter makes excuses: "He's busy. He has a lot of responsibilities. He loves me, but he gets distracted." She is covering the pain of not having a father who really cares for her by lying to herself.

Although such excuse making is understandable, it rarely helps a woman. It creates moments of painful disillusionment and empowers the father to continue hurting and shaming his daughter, particularly if she never puts up the necessary shield. Because she *wants* a caring father, she acts as if she *has* a caring father, and the cycle of hurt keeps rolling along.

If you want to grow into a healthy independence, you'd better be good at establishing the difference between fantasy and reality. Coming to grips with who your father really was and how he really treated you can be particularly difficult (and important) for a woman from a broken home. David Blankenhorn, president of the Institute for American Values, writes, "Because daughters of divorce often have a hard time finding out what their fathers are really like, they often experience great difficulty in establishing a realistic view of men in general, in developing realistic expectations, and in exercising good judgment in their choice of partner and in their relationships with men."[1]

Notice the breadth of the devastation of never coming to grips with your unmet father hunger. Blankenhorn says that you'll have a distorted view of men in general, making it more difficult to develop meaningful male friendships; you won't have realistic expectations of what your husband will be like or how he should act as a father; and you'll be challenged to make a good and wise decision about the type of man you should marry. In short, virtually every area of your life—work, home, marriage, and family—will be adversely affected if you don't get a better handle on how your father has affected you.

I often counsel women suffering from DADD. They can appear amazingly competent and professional on the outside, but when they finally let their guard down, they shake like scared bunnies. They often act like scared bunnies too. Young women who are from broken homes (or who had abusive fathers) are far more likely to experience affairs with older men as they search for the father they never had. These women frequently exchange sex in return for the cuddling, closeness, and masculine attention they never got at home.

The worst thing you can do in response to father hunger is to become promiscuous. That'll really throw your radar for a loop, creating an ever-worsening cycle of downward drift. Instead of getting sexual, you need to get analytical and evaluate how your father raised you. Did he overparent or underparent you?

Father Styles

Though fathering can be measured on a spectrum, for the sake of simplicity, let's look at the two poles: a father who overparents and a father who underparents.

The Overparenting Father

Instead of helping you form your own opinions, did your dad berate your ideas that differed from his ideas? Instead of encouraging you to become responsible, did he wittingly or unwittingly keep you dependent by giving you endless rules to follow and dozens of hoops to jump through? Did he encourage you to develop your strengths and abilities, or did he criticize and/or coddle you to such an extent that you don't believe you *have* any strengths or abilities?

A dad who overparents will eventually smother his daughter. He's positive he knows how his little girl should turn out, and he'll raise her to be like a seal that claps its flippers when Daddy holds out a fishy little morsel. When this happens, she will always seek her daddy's ever-elusive approval and have little or no confidence in herself.

Warning signs that you've been overparented include a serious lack of confidence and a childlike dependence. Has your husband ever suggested that he sometimes thinks he married a little girl who expects him to be the dad?

The long-term effects of overparenting can be severe. One study found that controlling, rejecting fathers may contribute to hysteria in adult women, leading to irrational angry outbursts, dependency and helplessness, and a tendency to use manipulative suicidal threats.[2] Overparented females frequently fail to develop the internal responsibility needed to succeed in life.

The Underparenting Father

Does this sound familiar? You're an eight-year-old girl who finally hears your dad walking through the door (two hours after dinner). You run up to greet him, excited that he's home. He gives you a quick hug, then says, perhaps quite firmly, "Now leave Daddy alone for a bit, Honey. I've had a long day at work." You wait until he changes his clothes and then sit beside him as he eats his dinner, but your mom says, "Now, Susie, let Daddy read the newspaper while he eats."

Dejected, you go back into the living room, but your eyes light up twenty minutes later when your dad walks in. Your heart sinks, however, when he immediately goes to his easy chair, picks up the remote, turns on the television, and once again tunes you out of his life.

If you felt like your dad's "shadow," always hovering for attention that you rarely received, you may well have had an underparenting dad. Underparenting dads place kids low on the ladder of priorities. Even when they're home—which doesn't tend to be a big priority—these dads are often someplace else mentally and emotionally. Their children are welcome to tag along, but the dads make little or no effort to enter their kids' worlds. They don't know what music their kids listen to, what shows they watch on television, or how they spend their afternoons. All they seem concerned about is that the kids "behave"—that is, they don't cause any trouble or commotion that would require the dads to expend a precious bit of their energy.

Children who are loved too little (victims of DADD) tend to respond to their fathers' distance by becoming overachievers in their vocations. The flip side is that their relationships are frequently a mess. Do you know how to succeed in the business world, but you don't have a clue about how to relate to men in social situations? When you're alone, are you sometimes overcome by a fear that unless you keep conquering new worlds, you're not really worth anything? In other words, is your self-esteem shot?

If the answer is yes, you probably had an underinvolved dad.

Getting Objective

To help you move from fantasy to reality, take a piece of paper, draw a line across it, and mark one end of the line "Overparenting Dad" and the other end "Underparenting Dad." Where on this line does your dad fit? Was he a responsible dad, actively involved in your life while also encouraging you toward independence? If he was, put him right in the middle. You're a lucky daughter. If you're tempted to put your dad near either end, then you know you've got some work to do before you reestablish an adult father-daughter relationship.

For a second exercise, take out another sheet of paper, and draw a line down the middle, creating two columns. In the left column, write "Characteristics of an Ideal Relationship with a Father." In the right column, write "Characteristics of My Real Relationship with My Father."

In the left column, dream about what you wish your relationship with your father was like—the longings of your heart, including affection, support, respect, and protection. In the right column, try to describe, as accurately as you can, your real relationship with your father. Don't gloss over painful areas. You need to see for yourself the size of the gap you need to overcome.

Don't be surprised if you sense a certain longing as you go through this exercise. You know the latent sense that you've always been missing something but you were never sure exactly what it was? Well, this is it. This is the father you've always wanted, pitted against the father you've always had.

Take some time to complete your list, even a week or more. Return to the list as you think of things to add, making it complete, getting a good understanding of what you desire and what you really have. There's no time limit on it; you're doing this for yourself.

After you've filled it out as much as you can, sit on it for a while. Let reality sink in and take root. There's no need to rush. If you've been living in the darkness for decades, it will take time for your emotional eyes to become adjusted to the light.

When you believe you have gained a certain measure of objectivity, pull out your list and ask yourself some hard questions: *Given who my father is, is a future relationship salvageable or reasonable? Is this a relationship that is worth pursuing, considering the cost? Am I getting myself into deeper trouble by hoping for more than I currently have?*

You have to get rid of the "man who never was" (your fantasy father) before you can make wise decisions about what you will pursue in the future. Here is one of the hardest statements I've ever had to make to a woman: "You know, the man you're describing to me will never be able to give you what you're seeking. In fact, if you approach him about it, things will probably get worse."

Leman's Law #11:
You have to get rid of the "man who never was"—your fantasy father—before you can make wise decisions about what kind of father-daughter relationship you will pursue in the future.

You may determine that even though your father has many faults, a future relationship with him is both possible and desirable. If you still believe the relationship is worth pursuing, you need to reestablish it on an adult basis.

Becoming an Adult Daughter

To pursue a new relationship with your real father, you must break out of the thinking that leads you to relate to him as child to man instead of woman to man. Doing this may take some courage on your part, but it's essential for you to draw clear guidelines. For example, if your father had a tendency to overparent—if he's the type of dad who smothered you and who, even though you're now twenty-eight, treats you as if you're twelve—you might try responding in this way:

"Dad, I appreciate your thinking of me, but you know, I just think it's healthier that if I need your help, I'll call you and ask for it. When you tell me how to do it without my asking, it goes back to how I felt as a little kid. Whenever I had anything to say, you sort of overrode it and I felt that I wasn't important. I felt so insignificant."

Be direct and forceful, but respectful. You've had time to emotionally adjust and reconsider how you are going relate to your father in the future. You'll need to extend the same grace to your father so that he can learn how to relate to you as an adult. You may have to express these thoughts several times before he gets the idea that you really have grown up.

If the relationship is estranged or a bit more distant than you would wish, I've found it helpful for a daughter to begin by writing her dad a letter. Write this letter carefully and gently. You might try something along these lines:

> Dear Dad:
>
> I just wanted to take some time out today to tell you how I feel about myself as it relates to you. I'm so thankful that you provided for us. I know you worked hard to put food on the table and keep a roof over our heads. I know that you and Mom had problems, but you went out of your way to make things as easy as possible for us to deal with that.
>
> While I am so grateful for these things, I feel it's only right to tell you that I also felt that I was never very important to you. I'm trying to think of a time that you looked at me and said, "I love you," or "I'm proud of you," but I can't.
>
> I never heard you say that you appreciated me for who I am. I can't think of a time when you really affirmed what I did.
>
> Dad, I'm thirty-six years old, and in a way I can't believe I'm writing this letter to you, but I want you to know that I still wish that things were, in fact, different between us. For a long time I've felt that something was missing in my life, and I've come to realize that something is a closer relationship with you. I'd like for us to reconnect as adults and have a relationship that both of us will enjoy.
>
> I know we see each other once in a while—for example, every

other Christmas—but if there's any way we can become closer, even at this late stage in life, I would consider it a privilege to learn more about who my dad is. Inside me there's still a little girl who continues to crave her dad's affirmation and love.

I'm using this letter to share with you that I really do love you. I know we've had our moments, but I'm willing to look past them if you are. In fact, I'd like to spend some significant time getting reacquainted.

That's why I want to invite you and Carol to come to our home for Thanksgiving. If you could arrive several days before and spend some extended time with us, that would be great. You've seen your grandchildren just twice, and I would really like them to get to know their grandfather.

Please let me know if you can make it.

Love,
Jennifer

Note that this letter *doesn't* blame your father for the failure of his first marriage. It does invite him to reestablish a broken or neglected relationship. He might respond; he might not. But you've done your part in helping to create the opportunity. The letter shows that though you have discarded a fictionalized view of your father, you are also eager to get to know your real-life father.

Some fathers will respond quite well to a letter like this; others may erupt and cut things off. There's no guarantee about your father's response. But if you want a relationship with your father, it's worth finding out whether your father is in the same position you are. That's much healthier than pretending to have a relationship that is all subterfuge.

What if your father is unwilling to have the relationship with you that you desire to have with him? Then it's time for you to change your childhood memories.

Changing Your Childhood Memories

Ashley is twenty-three and in a serious relationship with a young man. She is a Christian, as is her boyfriend, Don. Everything looks positive toward a rewarding marriage, but Ashley feels caught in the middle of her father's disapproval. Her dad thinks Don is a loser.

After a few minutes of casual conversation with her, I'm able to ask a question that rocks Ashley's world. "Ashley," I say, "have you ever known anyone who met with your father's approval?"

She doesn't immediately reply, but her lip quivers and she furiously attempts to compose herself. As the truth sinks in, Ashley finally whispers, "No." It hurts like a buzz saw for her to admit that, but she knows it's true. Now she finally knows that she knows it's true.

If you lived with a disapproving father, you must get rid of a model in which other people, including your dad, have to approve of you at every turn. If your life revolves around pleasing a father who isn't pleased by anybody, you're dooming yourself to failure.

I don't want to sound too harsh, but not everybody is going to like you. And, yes, encountering a disapproving individual will remind you of a father who constantly found fault with you. Your only solution is to learn to get over it. There is no magic formula. You are rejecting a lie—in this case, your father's disapproval of you and everyone else—and embracing a truth: If God can love you with all your wrinkles and shortcomings, what's wrong with your dad?

As a public speaker, I've had to learn this lesson. Some people attempt to build their sense of importance by tearing down the accomplishments of others, and sometimes these self-appointed critics attend my seminars. A few people have walked up to the microphone in front of several thousand people and challenged virtually everything I've said for the past sixty minutes.

Instead of getting irate, I've learned to say, "You know, you could be right. Next question?" When I respond in this way, the audience often erupts into spontaneous applause before the next person can ask a question. I think people respect that I am not captive to one person's displeasure or insistent on getting everyone to like me or agree with me. In my seminars, I offer my perspective based on my years in practice and my study of God's Word. People can take it or leave it.

Publishers have passed on some of my books that another publisher agreed to publish. In one gratifying instance, a book turned down by a publisher sold more than one hundred thousand copies *in six weeks* with a different publisher. Just because one person doesn't like, appreciate, or support what I'm doing isn't going to faze me because I've learned—as you must—that more often than not, the critics are wrong, even if they happen to go by the name of Dad.

> **Leman's Law #12:**
> Memories can be dead wrong.

I read an interesting article several years ago in which Hollywood actor Gene Hackman said he had learned to "change his childhood memories." His father abandoned him and his siblings at an early age, literally driving out of their lives in his car. Gene was an adult before he saw his father again, but even decades later his father refused to talk about what he had done.

Gene could have become bitter, but if he had done that, he would have forever been his father's emotional prisoner. Instead, Gene made a mature choice and "changed his childhood memories." He decided to discard the false image of a "superwonderful" entity in his life that, over the years, he had put on a pedestal. Instead, he accepted the fact that his dad was a deeply flawed, somewhat selfish person, a man like anyone else. Instead of pining for the approval of a dad who never was, he changed his memories to realize he had ached for the attention of a man who was too weak to offer the love and care Gene so desperately needed.

Changing memories can be hard to do, but it's vital. Your father is a human being, nothing more, nothing less. Nobody looks at him the way you do. At work, he's Joe Lunch Bucket, nobody special. His superhuman label is there by your design, and you can take off that label if you want to.

Memories can be dead wrong. The man you thought you knew may be very different from the man who really was. Evaluate those childhood assumptions, and discard the ones that don't fit within an adult's objective observations.

Getting objective, becoming an adult daughter, and changing your childhood memories are all effective strategies to reestablish a relationship with your dad. We could call these strategies your basic "defense." Now let's talk about going on the "offense," creatively confronting father hunger.

Creatively Confront Father Hunger

Three strategies will help you move on if you know that any hopes of a relationship with your biological father are dim at best. We could consider these your "offense." Father hunger can be met through turning toward a stand-in, through leaving your father and cleaving with your husband, and through finding the Father you're really looking for.

Turning Toward a Stand-in

"Susan" is in her mid-twenties. Her father left her mother when Susan was three years old, and her stepfather primarily raised her, though she paid regular visits to her biological father. Understandably, it was difficult for Susan to become emotionally involved with her stepfather, but she was fortunate that her mom had chosen a gentle, patient, and godly man for her second husband. This man loved Susan as much as she would let him.

Just a few years after she was married, Susan felt her hunger for father love increasing rather than decreasing (a fairly common phenomenon, by the way). She and her husband had moved out of state, and her biological father visited her when he was in town on business. Susan eagerly awaited his visit, but her heart sank when her father spent the entire time asking her why her younger sister (also his daughter) and he didn't have a relationship.

The cynical response, of course, would have been, "Well, it might have helped if you hadn't cheated on Mom and then left us when she was just a one-year-old." Instead, Susan silently grieved and waited for him to leave.

After that visit, Susan's father kept up the same old relationship: he didn't return e-mail or phone messages, but when *he* wanted to initiate, he poured buckets of guilt on her head, asking why his daughters weren't more affectionate, affirming, and responsive.

Susan was once again left with a void, which grew to such an extent that she sought counseling. She was old enough to begin making some decisions of her own, and one of those decisions was that she wanted to come to grips with the father hunger inside her.

In counseling, she was able for the first time to come to terms with the fact that her father had abandoned her and that he would probably never be able to give her what she wanted. She did this with resignation, not bitterness or anger.

Instead of turning against her father, Susan chose to turn toward her stepfather. She called him one night and put it this way: "I've come to realize that my dad doesn't want intimacy; he wants only my affection and approval."

> **Leman's Law #13:**
>
> Some dads don't want intimacy; they just want their daughters' affection and approval.

Her stepfather listened with tears in his eyes as she continued, "Dad [that's what she calls her stepfather], do you think you and I could have that intimate kind of relationship? Do you think we could figure out what it is like to connect as father and daughter?"

The stepfather made it quite clear that he would welcome such a relationship. When Susan came into town for the next visit, stepfather and daughter sat down alone at a table, looked each other in the eyes, and started talking. Neither knew where it would end up, but the daughter was determined to explore where that might be.

Let me tell you what is healthy about this situation. Susan is mature enough to realize that she can't get water out of a rock. Her biological father is an emotional black hole. He sucks other people into his insatiable need for approval and respect, and he is unwilling to give anything back. Susan will never receive what she wants from this man. The sooner she understands that, the better.

Next, taking stock, she realizes that she might have a second chance to experience a healthier father-daughter relationship with her stepfather. He isn't her biological father, and he came on the scene after she was eight years old, but she understands that this man is capable of giving. It might not be an ideal situation, but what Susan is doing is very wise.

Leman's Law #14:
Life often forces a woman to choose reality and the good over fantasy and the supposed best.

Just one word of warning. Women suffering from DADD tend to do no better picking stand-in fathers than they do husbands, which we talked about earlier. Make sure you apply the principles of Cognitive Self-Discipline—stop, look, and listen—as you seek to find a stand-in. (You'll read more about Cognitive Self-Discipline, or CSD, in Chapter 14.) You don't want to build a relationship with a substitute father that will bring the same damaging emotions associated with your childhood father.

Ultimately you will need to find the masculine presence you seek in your husband. To do this, you need to learn how to leave before cleaving.

Leaving and Cleaving

I can't overstate how important it is for a wife—particularly one with a substandard father—to learn how to leave and cleave. The leaving is essential for a healthy marriage.

Once you're married, whatever you have to do to get out from under your father's thumb, do it. That may mean settling for a less-than-ideal living situation. For instance, Sande's and my first apartment was in *a dormitory*. I was the head resident, and though we had our own room, essentially we lived with 360 guys. It was not our first choice, but the rent was free and this arrangement allowed us to live on our own, apart from our parents.

Especially if your father's negative imprinting has affected you, it is essential to get out from under his influence and start over afresh. Creating physical distance is one of the best ways to overcome the illusion of a father who never was. After you've been away and have begun to build a healthy relationship with your husband, you'll be better equipped to evaluate the way you and your father relate as adults. When your kids get older, I think it is healthy to move back near the grandparents and give your children a sense of heritage, but for a while and for some circumstances, moving away from your parents can be a very valuable experience.

Controlling men use their money and seeming generosity to keep others under their control. It's better to be poor and free to start a new life with your new husband than to have a brand-new house (or car or wardrobe) and still be under your father's thumb.

You can't cleave if you don't leave. Don't let a false image of your father get in the way of a real marriage. I've known many women who were raised by substandard fathers but who nevertheless wisely transferred that need for receiving male affirmation and approval to their husbands. As a result, they have become much stronger people and have enjoyed very happy marriages.

Another essential step—for every woman, not just those who have a difficult time relating to their earthly fathers—is to develop a deeper relationship with your heavenly Father.

Finding the Father You're Looking For

As part of a Bible study to help heal her wounds from having an abortion, Cheryl was asked, "What do you wish your earthly father had done for you?" She didn't have to think long. She dreamed of once again being a child, rocking in her dad's arms as his deep voice serenaded her. "I never heard my father sing, but the resonance in his voice was clear and soothing," she remembered.

Cheryl's relationship with her dad had been a rough one. Physical and verbal abuse marred her childhood. Rebellion characterized her teenage years. Even so, these factors did not dim her desire for her daddy's love, but her father wasn't able or willing to show it.

During a tough year of transition, Cheryl (in her early forties) received a card from a friend who sent her what seemed like a "curious" Scripture reference:

> The LORD your God in your midst,
> The Mighty One, will save;
> He will rejoice over you with gladness,
> He will quiet you with His love,
> He will rejoice over you with singing. (Zeph. 3:17)

Several times throughout the coming months, the same verse appeared on cards and letters addressed to her. It's such an unusual verse—not too many people scour the book of Zephaniah—that Cheryl took notice, but finally decided it must all be "coincidence."

After the arduous year ended with Cheryl leading a conference for more than six hundred people, she became physically, emotionally, and spiritually exhausted. "I felt as if I had been stretched to breaking," she remembered. She was staying at the Founders Inn in

Virginia Beach, Virginia, and trying to recover while enjoying a quiet meal with a few close friends.

Because she had directed the conference, Cheryl got to stay in one of the nicest rooms. It had a huge balcony overlooking a courtyard and pond. As Cheryl and her friends ate, they heard bagpipes begin to play a Scottish hymn outside in the courtyard.

"Have you ever heard 'Amazing Grace' on the bagpipes?" Cheryl asked her friend.

"Ewww. No, and I don't think I'd want to," her friend replied.

"It's the loveliest sound in the world," Cheryl insisted.

Once the bagpipe player finished the Scottish hymn, he walked to the edge of the pond, executed a military turn, and faced Cheryl and her friends in the balcony.

"My heart burst," Cheryl said. "I felt he was looking right at me. A moment passed, and then the chords of 'Amazing Grace' filled the air."

With tears in her eyes, Cheryl recounted, "My Father in heaven was singing to me. I knew He was comforting me and letting me know of His deep and abiding love for me. Many people were in the courtyard that day, but I know He was singing to me and showing His love, His tenderness, and His comfort."

Leman's Law #15:

You can't go back and give yourself a new earthly father, but you can find the comfort, love, and affirmation you crave from your daddy by looking heavenward and getting to know your spiritual Father.

The curious Scripture verse from Zephaniah—"He will rejoice over you with singing"—suddenly made great sense. Cheryl's heavenly Father was serenading His beloved daughter. Mesmerized, Cheryl took it all in.

"I sobbed," she said. "Years later, I'm still moved more than I can express when I recall that glorious day, the remarkable man in the kilt, and the amazing grace and love my heavenly Father has for me.

"My earthly father did not sing to me, read to me, or comfort me as a child. In that moment, for the first time in my life, it no longer mattered. God was, and is, the Father I've always yearned for."

You can't go back and give yourself a new earthly father. You can't re-create a man who refuses to change. But you can find the comfort, love, and affirmation you crave from your daddy by looking heavenward and getting to know your spiritual Father. He's eager to take you into His arms, coddle you, love you, and affirm you if only you'll point your eyes heavenward.

Unlike your earthly father, this Father has no limitations on His love. He can find very creative ways to let you know how much you mean to Him, and you'll experience freedom unlike any you've known before. I've encouraged many women to step in front of a mirror and say, "God, help me to love me as I know You love me." Doing this allows women to recapture the acceptance they never received from their earthly fathers. Some men are incapable of giving this acceptance, and it's no use dropping your bucket into a dry well and pulling up more sand.

Change wells! Drop your bucket and refresh yourself with what Jesus called "living water." Transfer your allegiance and sense of belonging from a man who will never be able to give you what you want—and who may derive a sadistic thrill from denying you what he knows you crave so desperately—and set yourself free by receiving from God what you've always desired.

Older diners sometimes display a sign that makes me chuckle: "In God We Trust. All Others Pay Cash." That's not a bad slogan for relationships. When you start putting people—and even a father—on pedestals, you set them up to let you down.

Your father hunger is actually a longing to reconnect with the God who made you, your spiritual Father in heaven. Get to know this Father, and you'll go a long way toward having the strength and resources to get to know your earthly father.

A Daughter's Self-Defense

A few years ago I learned the true meaning of pain. I thought I knew what pain was all about until a chalklike object about the size of a large, twenty-five-cent gum ball gave me an entirely new perspective.

It was a gallstone wreaking havoc inside my body. The doctors knew it had to come out, so they admitted me into the hospital, and my family dutifully gathered around me. Then they sat in the waiting room while the pernicious little sucker was removed.

Sande and the kids were in the middle of eating their Burger King lunches when the doctor walked out to talk to them. "Want to see it?" he asked in a cheery voice.

Before he could decipher the white color that blanketed the faces of all the Leman females, the surgeon laid out my gallbladder (that gets taken out, too) and the brown-and-white stone that had caused all the trouble.

My family made it quite clear to me that they could have lived very well-adjusted lives without ever seeing their father's gallbladder and gallstone. Some things about your dad you just don't need to know.

> **Leman's Law #16:**
> Every father has his ugly realities, his prejudices, and his failures. Take a difficult step and forgive him.

We have been spending a good bit of time beating up on dads, but let's turn a corner here. Your father might have overparented or underparented you. You need to know that and deal with it. But there isn't a single woman who has ever been raised by a perfect parent. That woman doesn't exist. Every father has his ugly realities, his prejudices, his failures, his own way of coping. You don't necessarily want to see any of them or witness them, but as an adult, you must. And then you need to take an even more difficult step and forgive him.

You're not perfect, and you can't expect your dad to be perfect either. Your dad isn't God. The closer you grow toward God, ironically enough, the easier you'll find it to accept your father with all his faults.

"But, Dr. Leman," a woman may ask me, "why must I forgive my dad? Didn't you hear what he did to me?"

"Of course, I did," I'll say. "That's *why* you need to forgive."

I would never fault a woman if she faces real difficulty forgiving her father for his painful absence or, even worse, his outright abuse. But a woman who wants to be a follower of Christ has no choice but to forgive. Jesus said we are to forgive "seventy times seven."

Part of the reason for the need to forgive—and this is what I really want you to understand—is self-preservation. A woman who maintains a bitter spirit pollutes her own soul. An article in the January 10, 2000, issue of *Christianity Today* examined how social scientists are discovering the therapeutic value of forgiveness—that is, the first person served by forgiveness *is the one who does the forgiving!*

Dr. Glen Mack Harnden writes that forgiveness "releases the offender from prolonged anger, rage, and stress that have been linked to physiological problems, such as cardiovascular diseases, high blood pressure, hypertension, cancer, and other psychosomatic illness."[1]

> **Leman's Law #17:**
> Physically, spiritually, and emotionally, forgiveness is an act of self-defense. It saves us from the destructive disease of bitterness.

By offering forgiveness, you stop someone else's sin and infection from becoming your own.

I'll confess, extending forgiveness is not any easier for me than it is for you. Jesus' "seventy times seven" is an ideal I'm working toward. My usual limit is three! If the same person does the same thing to me three times, I'm tempted to become a spiritual umpire and say, "Three strikes! You're outta here!"

I've come across a truth that cuts against what most Christian teachers might say. I don't believe you should "forgive and forget." I'm a staunch proponent of "forgive and remember."

Forgive and Remember

If you've ever played golf and hit a nice drive off the tee, you might have experienced what I have. Once you get to your ball and look back, you say to yourself, "Wow! Did I hit it that far?" For some reason, the distance seems longer as you look back.

A spiritual lesson is evident here. When I "forgive and remember," I'm able to look back and see the great progress I've made. During the ordeal and process of forgiveness, I might have felt as if I was going backward or as if I was caught in a stream's eddy, going around in circles but not making any progress.

There is something profound about baby steps. You take life and emotional pain one minute at a time and keep moving forward. Beautiful cathedrals are built one brick at a time. Difficult forgiveness is maintained one second at a time. If someone says to you today, "Forgive your father right now so that you can give him a hug and tell him how much you love him," doing that may seem no less impossible for you than someone dumping a pile of bricks on your front yard and saying, "Now, build a cathedral."

It takes time. At first, you may have to keep renouncing your anger. You may need to remind yourself that Jesus died for all sinners, including your father. Don't worry about the enormity of the job. Just focus on getting through the present moment. Your attitude should mirror that of a woman who was found lying on a beach. She was the lone survivor of a shipwreck, and her rescuer heard the emaciated, exhausted woman still muttering, "Just one more stroke. Just one more stroke. Just one more stroke."

"Forgive and remember" encourages you to look back and see your progress as well as that of your father. It's probably not realistic for you to expect your dad to do a 180-degree turn and suddenly become the father you've always wanted. That's why you need to remember the following:

- The actions that get you in trouble with this man
- The lies you told yourself about your past or your father
- The credit you deserve for the effort you've made
- The progress your father has made (if any)

That's a lot to remember!

And this point cannot be overemphasized: Become satisfied with imperfect results. Too many women set their expectations so high that they guarantee failure. Accept the best that you can salvage. Don't let the ideal become the enemy of what you *can* have.

This is all part of the most vital step—move on.

Move On

During the Civil War, more men died of infection following a wound than from the actual injury. Many women today suffer the same casualty. Their lingering response of unforgiveness, bitterness, and resentment—not the original offense—does them in.

After you've forgiven your father, you need to move on. Maybe your father didn't show much affection, but maybe he also had it really tough, caught in a job he didn't like but forced to stay there to pay the bills. Maybe his education topped out at the eighth grade (like my dad's), and he came from a family that didn't show much affection. Given his background, he might have been the best father he could be. I say all of this not to excuse your father, but to help you understand him.

During a counseling session in my office, there is usually a defining moment. I'll listen to a client tell me her tales of woe and how she had it so tough, and I'll sit there and empathize with her—for a while. Eventually I'll say, "Allison, I accept the fact that life has been unfair to you. You certainly have had more than your share of challenges. Now, what are you going to do about it? Are you going to suck it up and move on, or are you going to wallow in self-pity the rest of your life and use this as an excuse for your inability to go forward?"

Using this approach helps a woman prepare for that fateful call. You need to do something vital before your father dies.

Prepare for a Fateful Call

Arlene was in the middle of a television program when the phone rang. She contemplated letting the machine answer it. *It's probably just a telemarketer*, she thought. But a ringing phone is hard to ignore, so Arlene got off the couch and received the call that penetrated her warm, comfortable world with an arctic blast.

"Arlene, it's Mom. I'm at the hospital. Honey, prepare yourself. Your father just died."

You may prefer to write the old man off, just take him out of your life, and for a while, you may need to do that. But I urge you to think very carefully about doing it for any length of time. Here's why: the day is probably going to come when you receive a phone call very similar to the one placed to Arlene. There will be a moment in your life when you can no longer relate to Dad; he'll be gone, and at that moment, any number of emotions will be released.

Years ago, a Christian writer wrote a piece for *Guideposts* magazine that still tears me up.[2] Sue is a registered nurse who was caring for a seriously ill man named Mr. Williams. As she checked on him, Mr. Williams asked Sue to call his daughter.

"Of course I'll call her," Sue said, but that wasn't good enough for Mr. Williams. "Will you call her right away—as soon as you can?" he pleaded.

"I'll call her the very first thing," Sue assured him.

Just before she left the room, Mr. Williams asked Sue for a pencil and a piece of paper. She found a pen and a scrap of stationery and walked out to call the daughter.

As soon as the nurse dialed the number she had been given and said "heart attack," she heard a loud scream on the other end of the line. "No! He's not dying, is he?"

"His condition is stable," Sue assured her.

"You must not let him die," Janie, the daughter, begged. "My daddy and I haven't spoken in almost a year." Janie explained that they had fought over a boyfriend. The argument ended with Janie running out of the house. Many times she had thought about calling her father and asking for forgiveness, but it never seemed to be the "right" time.

"The last thing I said to him was, 'I hate you,'" Janie explained through deep sobs. Then in a rush of emotion, the bereaved daughter promised her father's nurse, "I'm coming. Now! I'll be there in thirty minutes."

Sue hung up the phone but found it unusually difficult to concentrate, so she finally walked into Mr. Williams's room. He lay frighteningly still. The nurse reached for his wrist and, to her horror, couldn't find a pulse. Immediately she put out the alert: "Code 99. Room 712. Code 99. Stat!"

Mr. Williams had suffered a cardiac arrest.

In a furious rush, Sue began breathing air into Mr. Williams's lungs, then performed CPR. *Oh God*, she prayed, *his daughter is coming. Don't let it end this way.*

Doctors and nurses rushed in, many carrying emergency medical equipment. A physician inserted a tube into Mr. Williams's mouth. Nurses plunged syringes of medicine into the IV. Sue busied herself by connecting a heart monitor.

Her heart seemed still when she was unable to detect a single beat. The lead physician cried out, "Stand back," and took the paddles from Sue to shock Mr. Williams's heart back to life. One hit. Two hits. Three hits.

Nothing.

Finally the doctors and nurses gave each other knowing looks. The lead physician shook his head. A nurse unplugged the oxygen.

Mr. Williams was dead.

When Sue left the room, she saw a young woman slumped against the wall. A doctor had already delivered the information.

"Such pathetic hurt reflected from her face," Sue wrote. "Such wounded eyes."

Sue accompanied Janie into a quiet room, where the daughter assured the nurse, "I never hated him. I loved him."

Janie then asked to see her daddy, so Sue led her to Mr. Williams's bed. Janie buried her face in her dead father's sheets. As Sue backed up, her hand fell on the scrap of paper she had handed to her patient just moments before. A man's scrawl read:

> My dearest Janie,
>
> I forgive you. I pray you will also forgive me. I know that you love me. I love you too.
>
> Daddy

"The note was shaking in my hands as I thrust it toward Janie," Sue wrote. "She read it once. Then twice. Her tormented face grew radiant. Peace began to glisten in her eyes. She hugged the scrap of paper to her breast."

The father's last act was to give his daughter a priceless gift—reconciliation. In the face of death, both father and daughter were willing to forgive. When both realized that time on this earth is not unending, they were desperate to make things right.

Many stories don't end quite so peaceably. Death can creep in unexpectedly, like a cruel and vindictive tyrant, whisking the father away before reconciliation can apply its healing balm.

Don't let this happen to you!

For their own health, if for no other reason, some women need to know they've really given the father-daughter relationship their all. Even if a renewed relationship isn't possible—at least not the relationship they had hoped for—they derive comfort from the knowledge that they explored every possible avenue. Something about this makes the loss easier to handle.

Someday this father of yours who has been such a thorn in your side is going to die. Statistically speaking, it is far more likely that you will bury him than he will bury you. Since you know that day is coming, ask yourself, *Is there anything I need to say to him? Is there any unfinished business I shouldn't put off any longer?*

A danger of leaving unfinished business is that we tend to take out our unresolved anger and hurt on those we love. We make our own children (and especially our spouses) pay for the sins of our fathers and *thereby play a role in perpetuating our fathers' sins.*

A woman named Cheryl Jakubowski—whom we met in the previous chapter when God "sang" to her—was determined not to let that happen.

Accept Life's Surprises

After you've come to terms with the fact that your experience with your father wasn't the best, life may still surprise you.

Cheryl took the typical route of a daughter who lacked affirmation from her father. "I decided to take the better way to receive attention and acknowledgment from my father," she said. "I decided I would earn it. I would be successful, make money, become self-sufficient, win his approval, and feel his love."

A particular sore spot was that her dad showed more tenderness to his cats than he did to her. In spite of all of Cheryl's accomplishments and successes, she had never once heard her dad affirm her or tell her he was proud of her. For a time, she needed to create a separation between her and her parents. The reunion, however, was sweet. "My father saw me and ran toward me, and I ran to him." But even then, her dad couldn't be completely affirming.

"When he began to cry as I did, he pushed me away and suggested I see my mother. It was overwhelming for him, and the emotions were too close to the surface for his comfort."

Several months later, her dad was diagnosed with lung cancer. Cheryl became the devoted daughter, sitting with her father, holding his hand, bringing him fun little treats, such as a covered coffee cup when his hand wasn't steady enough to grasp an open one.

And then an amazing thing happened. As Cheryl listened to her father moan through his pain, she started wishing she could bear it for him.

"The man I had hated and wanted to have punished—I finally loved as he was."

Near the end, as Cheryl's dad slipped ever closer to death, father and daughter started talking as they had never talked before. Cheryl was shocked to hear the self-hatred in her dad's voice, and she realized that he had spent a good bit of his life hating everyone—including himself.

Cheryl asked her father, "Who do you think God is?"

"A big guy who is probably very mad at me," her dad answered.

They talked some more, and then Cheryl asked her father if he would like to know Jesus in a personal way.

Her dad said yes, and Cheryl led him in a prayer of confession, repentance, and forgiveness.

That would have made Cheryl's day—*lifetime*—right there, but there was more to come. In virtually the last words she heard her father utter to her (he died shortly after this visit), he looked his grown daughter in the eye, and the emaciated man, who had been a Christian for all of five minutes, finally uttered the words his daughter had waited a lifetime to hear.

"Cheryl," he said, "I am so proud of you."

She felt a sense of completeness she had never known before. Not only had her dad said he was proud of her—and she could clearly see in his eyes that he was sincere—but the two of them, treating each other as adults, would be able to spend an eternity in heaven getting reacquainted.

I can't promise you that you'll experience what Cheryl experienced. Not every story has so difficult a beginning and so happy an ending. But Cheryl's willingness to move on, forgive, and accept her real dad rather than hide behind a fantasy dad paid big dividends in her life. Even if her dad hadn't come around, the process Cheryl went through would have given her a much more well-adjusted life.

Hatred has never healed anyone. Wallowing in misery has never produced happiness. You might have hated many things or even everything about your father, but what are you going to do with those things today? Will you carry them into the grave and lie for the rest of eternity in your bitterness, or will you risk the possibility that Jesus knew what was best for us when He said we should forgive seventy times seven?

The choice is yours.

7

The Strong Man Stumbles

That's not my dad. I don't know who he is, but that's not my dad."

Leslie peered through the window and couldn't imagine that the 138-pound invalid body lying in front of her once housed her 200-pound dad. This man, too weak to take a breath on his own, once carried her and her sister through 90 percent of a three-mile hike. When Leslie was five years old, she thought her father could fix anything—her bike, her roller skates, the family car, and the television set.

Now he looked helpless, being pricked and prodded and poked by all kinds of medical personnel who wrote little scribbles on his chart and walked out of the room shaking their heads.

The few wisps of hair that barely covered his head were mockeries of the full, thick bush that once crowned him. And his hands. You could never see his veins before.

Who *was* this man?

Watching the strong men in their lives reduced through the indignity of age and disease is a sobering travail, but it is one that most daughters must eventually encounter.

The Great Reversal

Frank is a World War II vet. He built his family's home with his own hands and worked for years in a variety of blue-collar jobs. He frequently worked overtime in late winter so his wife could buy his three little girls new Easter dresses every year. Though his daughters always suspected he secretly wished for a son who would be as rugged as he, Frank went out of his way to show his daughters how delighted he was that they were girls.

His wife died five years ago. Since then, Frank's daughters have stopped by "when in the neighborhood," even though not one lives or works within a thirty-mile radius.

"It's amazing how often you all are out of town," he told them one holiday, and all the daughters shared knowing looks. Frank pretended not to notice.

Recently Frank was delighted to receive a call from his oldest. It seemed like only yesterday when he had spent thirty minutes tramping through the backyard with a flashlight to find a small toy that she had lost earlier in the day and couldn't sleep without. Now she was an attorney, billing her hours at sums that made Frank's head spin.

And here she was, taking time out of her busy day to call him.

At first, they talked about the weather, the Chicago Cubs' draft picks, and the political situation in Washington, D.C. Nothing personal, and Frank soon realized his daughter had nothing personal to share. Then almost as an afterthought, she said, "Oh, by the way, did you take your new medicine this morning?"

Frank saw through the change in her tone of voice. That was the real purpose of her call. The doctor had given him a new prescription, and Frank's daughter wanted to make sure he wasn't forgetting to take it.

The truth hit him like a Hulk Hogan body slam. Years ago he worried over whether this same daughter was brushing her teeth before she went to bed. Now she was concerned about whether he was taking his medicine.

Thirty years make a big difference.

Because I'm an older dad (Lauren was born when I was forty-nine), I've grown acutely aware that my little girl will, in all likelihood, one day care for me—whether or not I want her to. Though I can carry her in one arm today, three decades hence she'll shake her head and say, "Now, Dad, you know that's not good for you."

Few things are more difficult in life than the great reversal. It is truly as hard for fathers to become the children as it is for the children to become the parents. If you want to relate to your father for a lifetime, however, you must accept this change and prepare for it. Your relationship with your father must evolve as both of you get older. This change presents new opportunities and new challenges.

Your Relationship Must Evolve

A friend was working with some colleagues on a newsletter for Christians that integrated faith and business. They were elated when one of them finally got in touch with an extremely distinguished and accomplished executive. This legendary Christian businessman and guru, who was in his late seventies, was almost impossible to track down because he closely guarded his privacy.

Much to my friend's dismay, the executive said he was "tired and bored" talking about business—he wanted to talk about his grandkids! Not at all surprised, I chuckled when I heard this story. It's almost a cliché for the ambitious, cutthroat young executive who ignores his children to grow into a grandfather who suddenly delights in a tiny human being more than he does boardroom politics.

> **Leman's Law #18:**
> As dads get older, they tend to mellow.

Perhaps your father spent his thirties, forties, fifties, and sixties on an ambitious assault to prove to the world that he mattered. In his seventies, you may very well find a far more mellow man who suddenly has time to sit down and talk with you and looks forward to your phone calls.

Much of this mellowing has to do with that pesky little chemical we've being talking about in this entire book: testosterone. As men age, the testosterone level in their bodies decreases, which usually means they become less ambitious and more relational. The level of this change will vary from man to man, but it is a common phenomenon.

I didn't have to wait until my sixties to mellow out, however. What mellowed me out as much as anything was watching my dad age. I became very aware that life is a series of choices. Grand gestures aren't nearly as important as consistent decisions. The little choices—going to the bar to shoot darts instead of getting home forty-five minutes earlier to play with our daughters—ultimately define our existence and the relationships we build. The same is true for you. Whether you decide to write that letter to your dad or take ten minutes out of your busy day to call him will greatly affect how close the two of you remain as adults.

If you've seen a father die, you know what I'm about to tell you: Life is shorter than we think, and people are more important than things. When we face the inevitable pressures of life and its constant demands, we'll never regret erring on the side of family. But thirty- and forty-year-old men can be notoriously shortsighted in this regard.

Though your father probably won't use this language, you may matter much more to him as he gets older. Once he sees how pitifully unfulfilling achieved ambition is apart from meaningful relationships, that hard heart of his is likely to grow soft.

Jimmy Johnson, a former coach of the Miami Dolphins, once allegedly told the press that he was leaving his wife because she was getting in the way of football. A decade later, he announced that he was quitting football to spend more time with his family.

Listen, *dads change.* When this happens, you have a tremendous opportunity. You might have initiated a conversation ten or five years ago and found your father unwilling to revisit your relationship. Don't assume he'll always feel that way. For your own sake, be willing to occasionally revisit these sensitive communications.

As your father's body breaks down, he's going to realize a horrible truth: In one sense, we all die alone. We may have our families around us, but we enter death as individuals. This glimpse of mortality can counteract the testosterone-laden, tough-guy, independent act that too many men have spent years cultivating and send them scurrying toward the shelter of the family they have ignored for years.

A sad reality is that when many fathers do this, some daughters refuse to respond. They bitterly hold seventy-year-old fathers responsible for sins they committed in their forties. That's understandable—they *are* the same persons, after all. But what is to be gained by refusing to let their fathers grow?

Your dad doesn't fault you for spitting up on him or for dirtying your diapers when you were a baby. He was fully aware of the elements of an infant's development. Can you provide the same understanding for a man as he grows out of his ambition? I know it's a different situation. You were a baby, and those acts were "unwillful" events without any moral choice involved. On the other hand, your dad was a grown adult making conscious choices.

You can either impale your dad on this distinction or use it to convince yourself that maybe you ought to give the guy another chance. If you refuse to let the relationship evolve, you'll never have more than you have now. If you are willing to forgive, there's a possibility—though not a certainty by any means—that you'll be able to enjoy a deeper father-daughter relationship than you've ever known.

The Great Temptation

The great reversal provides a great temptation. This is, after all, your chance to get back at your father and make him pay for all he's done wrong. If he has been entrusted to your care and you have legal power over him, you can make his life miserable.

You can treat him like a child, just as he treated you like one. You can demean him, shame him, or ignore him. The tables are turned now.

Resist the temptation. Go the opposite way and do your best to provide your dad with as much independence as possible. Honor him as your father, even if he wasn't a very good one.

Once again, this activity is self-preserving. You have the ability to pass on a legacy of resentment and abuse, or you can pioneer a new spirit of care, compassion, and respect. If you can't do it for your father's sake, do it for your children's sake—and your own.

> **Leman's Law #19:**
> Your kids didn't see how your father treated you when you depended on him, but they will see how you treat your father now that he is dependent on you.

As your dad ages, you will eventually face the most difficult evolution of all—relating to your dad *after* he has died.

Don't Ever Get Over It

It was a sensitive time for me. A well-known television celebrity had invited me to appear on her show. As we talked off camera, I learned that her father had passed away recently. She told me she was having real problems "getting over it."

"I hope you don't *ever* get over it," I said.

"What are you talking about?"

"Grief isn't a book with a beginning and an end," I explained. "It's like the tide. It keeps coming back with the seasons, though sometimes unpredictably. We wake up and it's there, and we have to deal with it."

"That makes so much sense," she said.

Unfortunately, people are often at their worst when somebody dies, especially when somebody dies suddenly. "You'll get over it" is a common—and cruel—refrain.

Three months or three years might have passed, and we'll find ourselves mourning anew. Well-meaning but hurtful friends say, "Don't you think it's time you got over that? It's been three years!"

What a terrible thing to say! Our fathers live within us. They aren't things we get over; they are influences and presences that will be with us until we die. How many times have you told yourself, *I'll never do what my father did*, just before you do exactly that with your children?

There's a positive side. If your father affirmed you, if you really felt loved by him, you are always going to be able to sense where someone has done you wrong or is attempting to abuse you. You'll also have the backbone to stand up for yourself and say, "Wait a minute! I don't buy this! I'm not going to allow you to treat me this way." In your words, if you listen carefully, you'll hear your father's tone.

Because your dad's indelible imprint—positive or negative—is too strong to be obliterated by physical absence, it is *vital* that you keep your father alive in your heart so that you can continue to grow in spite of or because of him.

Keep Your Dad Alive

At a conference in Ohio where I was speaking, a pastor was sitting behind me. All of a sudden, the pastor got up and left. Talking to the audience, I tried my best to think of what I might have said wrong, something that perhaps offended the pastor, but I couldn't come up with anything. Everybody had seen him leave, so it was quite an awkward situation.

Afterward, I found the pastor in tears. He had just lost his dad, and something in my talk about a dad's influence had cut him to the core. He had to get up and leave, he explained apologetically, or else break down in front of his congregation.

"Dr. Leman," he said, "sometimes I still talk to my dad. I hold up his picture as I sit on my bed and have conversations with him."

He paused, then asked me, "Is that okay?"

"I hope so," I replied, "because I do it all the time. I probably talk to my dad more now that he's dead than I ever did when he was alive!"

Talking to a dead parent is a natural thing to do. You miss him so much, it's human nature to say, "Gee, Dad, I really wonder what you would suggest I do now." Or "Boy, I really wish you could see your granddaughter dressed in her wedding gown. She's so lovely, and she's got Mom's eyes. It really hurts that you're not here to see her." Or "This is such a funny cartoon. I wish you were here so that I could read it to you. You always loved *Peanuts*, and I know you would enjoy this one."

When you talk to him, you may feel his presence. He may seem so close to you, you can almost feel his arms wrapping themselves around you.

Every April 25, I purposefully make my sister Sally cry. That day is our dad's birthday, and I know Sally still misses him terribly. As her younger brother, I have the responsibility to lovingly tease her. I can do a dead-on impersonation of our father, so I give Sally a father-daughter birthday call.

Donning our father's voice, I say, "Hello there, Wiener Legs. (That's what Dad always called her.) I'm just up here in heaven wondering what you're doing. Today is the big day, and I checked the mailbox and there was nothing from you. I thought you'd at least send the old man a couple of bucks. (Dad always talked about money.) They've got all this gold up here, but no money.

"Listen, Sally, I'd love to talk some more but I got to go to choir practice. I love ya."

One time Sally called back in tears and said, "Oh, you're so . . ." She couldn't finish the sentence. The best gift I could have given her was keeping her daddy alive, if only for a few short sentences.

I now do the same thing to my mom. "Hey, May," I call out in his accent, "where are my gray pants? I can't find them up here in the clouds and thought you could give me a hand."

These calls probably tear my sweet mom's heart out, but in a good way. My dad could never find anything without my mom's help, and I know just how to make him come down from heaven for a few brief, but precious, minutes.

Our desire to bury our memories with our parents is a futile attempt to run from pain. It hurts to see loved ones go, even when we know they're going to heaven. But we can recreate the joy they brought us and relearn the lessons they passed on when we keep them alive. Let's take the high road, the more mature path, and honor our dads by remembering them.

That may be the most important father-daughter evolution of all.

Now that we've looked at how profoundly you've been affected by your father, let's turn our attention to the man to whom your father helped lead you (either directly or indirectly): your husband.

PART 3

Your Husband: He Can Be Handy Around the House, but I'm Not Sure He Goes with the Furniture

Give Him Some Credit . . . and Some Time!

In this chapter, I'm going to tell you how you can meet your husband halfway. If I were writing this book for a man, I'd lay out the most important principles for him to learn, but since this book is written for you, we're going to talk about how a woman can better relate to her husband.

Behind many marital conflicts lie numerous misunderstandings regarding gender differences. Maybe your experience has been like that of Jean Kerr, who once wrote, "Marrying a man is like buying something you've been admiring for a long time in a shop window. You may love it when you get it home, but it doesn't always go with everything else in the house."[1]

The guy you dated looked pretty good—until you had to live with him. Now he seems like an alien from a distant planet, and you wonder how the two of you will ever make it.

Remember that I said boys' brains have much less sensory awareness than girls' brains? Well, the same is true of men. One wife in her early forties (we'll call her "Sue") told me how she became frustrated with her husband's amazing ability to live with debris on the floor. Sue suspected he didn't even see it.

One morning, Sue noticed that there was an empty toilet paper roll lying on the floor in one section of the master bathroom (this section, incidentally, is rather small—about six feet by six feet). She decided to conduct an experiment. Sue dated the toilet paper roll and then placed it back exactly where she found it. She wanted to see how long it would take her husband, Craig, to pick it up.

An entire week went by, and every morning Sue woke up, checked the bathroom, and discovered that the toilet paper roll was still there, lying on the floor. A month went by, two months, three months, then four months—an entire season! Sue had found the toilet paper roll the day before Halloween, and it was two weeks past Valentine's Day.

"Enough is enough!" she said. When Craig came home from work, Sue walked him into the bathroom and said, "I've been conducting a test. Do you have any idea what the test might be?"

Craig looked around. "You didn't paint the walls, did you?"

"No."

"The floor's the same, isn't it?"

"Yes."

"I'm sorry, I—"

Sue lost her patience. "The *toilet paper roll!* Didn't you notice the toilet paper roll on the floor? Look! I dated it! October 30. It's been lying here for four months!"

Craig shrugged his shoulders. "I'm sorry. I guess I just didn't see it."

"Wendy," another married woman, conducted a test of her own. She became increasingly frustrated that her husband, Allen, acted as if she was the only one who could buy toothpaste. One time, she let Allen keep squeezing and squeezing a virtually empty tube, wondering when he would eventually get the clue and buy some toothpaste on his own.

Finally Allen came downstairs one evening and said, "Wendy? I can't get any more toothpaste out of the tube, and the girls need to brush their teeth. Do we have a new tube?"

"I don't know," Wendy said. "Have you bought any lately?"

Allen was about as perplexed as a husband could be. "No," he chortled, as if buying toothpaste was the most bizarre thing he could ever imagine doing.

"Then I guess we must be out," Wendy replied.

Allen could tell by Wendy's tone that something was up, so he said, "How about if I go buy some?"

"That's a great idea," Wendy replied.

At least, she *thought* it was a great idea until he came home with, in Wendy's words, "*Galactic Blue Bubblemint Star Wars Toothpaste!*"

I have to confess as a man, I wasn't sure what the problem was. After all, she wanted Allen to buy the toothpaste, didn't she?

"Have you ever had to clean that stuff up?" Wendy half-yelled at me in reply. "That blue gunk sticks to *everything!*"

When Wendy buys toothpaste, she naturally thinks, *What toothpaste will make the least mess?* When Allen buys toothpaste, he thinks, *What toothpaste will make the kids the happiest?*

These misunderstandings happen in *every* marriage. It's part of the great gap that exists between what a woman values and what a man values. Thus, if we are going to get back "on plot," both sexes need to move toward each other with increased understanding, which is what I hope to provide for you in the next several chapters.

As a beginning, I'd like to urge you to give your husband a little more credit and a little more time.

Give Him a Break!

As I was writing this book, I came across a small story in the newspaper about a woman who had struck it rich with the lottery. She somehow managed to avoid the publicity and quietly divorced her husband, who had no idea that the woman leaving him was now a millionaire.

This story feeds into the fears of many men. If our wives didn't need our financial contributions, would they stay? Will they use us until they no longer need us and then discard us without a care?

I know you may be saying, "Hey, Leman! That's just what men do! We women bear their children, cook their meals, and slave over them for years until they become rich and leave us for younger trophy wives!"

Yes, that's true. There is no denying that throughout history, men have run over women. And I wouldn't argue that many men still do that today. The old adage "A man may work from sun to sun, but a woman's work is never done" is still probably true. Men tend to have much more compartmentalized lives. Women, especially stay-at-home moms, live, work, make love, and cook in their "offices"; they never "go home." And those who work outside the home do a majority of the housework. I'll be the first to admit that this situation isn't fair.

Even so, a growing number of men are making great strides. Professional basketball coach Danny Ainge recently announced his retirement, saying he wants to spend more time with their families. Dick Vermeil, the head coach of the Super Bowl Champion St. Louis Rams, announced his retirement, saying he wanted to get to know his grandchildren. Many men are taking an increasingly large share of the housework and childcare responsibilities.

Women can help the process along by giving us a little more credit. I know it's difficult to do when we have so many faults, but try to look beyond where we are to where we've come from. Yes, we have quite a ways to go, but most of us are making progress, aren't we?

Leman's Law #20:

When you get frustrated with men, don't just look at where we are; look at where we've come from.

In spite of our "caveman" reputation, most men get a lot of psychological jollies out of being providers, but many men, when they finally become honest with me in my office, admit to feeling unappreciated. I know, you do, too, but one of the best ways to emotionally emasculate a man is to take him for granted. If that's your aim, it's pretty easy to do. Don't even think about thanking him for working hard, being faithful to you, or spending time with the family. Just assume that he will do this gladly. He *may* keep doing it, but you will have robbed him of tremendous motivation.

As society tries out new roles for men and women, the signals can become tremendously confusing. Take the abortion issue, for instance. What is a man supposed to do when a woman he has slept with gets pregnant? According to the liberal-leaning women's groups, his politically correct response is to do *whatever the woman wants him to do.* If she wants to have an abortion, he should pay for it and keep his opinions to himself. If the woman doesn't want to have an abortion, he should gladly support that child for the rest of his life. If the woman wants to place the child for adoption, the man is expected to sign the papers without hesitation.

Do you see the problem here? The man is supposed to be more involved at home, but in this situation, he is not supposed to be involved at all unless the woman wants him to be involved. The women's groups are saying that there is no "objective" male response. Being a "responsible male" has been turned into doing whatever the woman wants you to do. Don't have your own opinion; just follow along.

We weren't made this way! It's confusing. And it's contributing to mixed signals at home.

Stay-at-home moms may not realize the pressure men face as they try to support a family. Because of some good teaching that challenges Christian men to become more like servants and less like tyrants, many wives have increased expectations for their husbands. Not only are men supposed to attend morning Bible studies, but they're also supposed to get home in time for dinner, spend time alone with each child, date their wives once a week, and earn enough money so that their wives can stay home with their young children.

This is a heavy load, and some Christian men start to resent it. One woman derided her husband, "You didn't act like this in college." He angrily retorted, "I wasn't supporting five people when I was in college!" Although men shouldn't use this as an excuse, the man was making a valid point. There's a lot of pressure on a man today, particularly the sole breadwinner. Bringing home enough to support a family so that the wife can stay home is becoming more and more difficult—and too many women take it for granted.

While we men get a lot of psychological fulfillment from providing for our families, it is far more emotionally fulfilling to have that provision *recognized*. There's a little boy inside every man who is pining for someone to say, "Good job!"

The next time you see your husband, you can give him a tremendous gift, and it won't cost you a dime. Tell him, "Thank you so much for . . . ," and list three or four things that you typically take for granted.

Besides giving her husband a little more credit, a wife, especially a young one, could give her husband a little more time.

Give Him More Time

It took me ten years to learn how to be married. I doubt that I'm an exception. When a guy gets married in his early twenties, it will take *years*, not months, for him to learn how to be selfless and considerate and to place the needs of his ego below the welfare of his wife.

Some men expect their wives to pick up where their mothers left off. Years later, they'll finally get a clue that their wives would like helpmates too; their wives would appreciate a hand around the house; their wives would like to be put first just once, be allowed to go out for lunch or dinner while their hubbies stay home with the little ones.

The exception may be a man who gets married in his early thirties after having lived away from home. This man—if he lived on his own—usually has a more independent streak and is better able to care for himself.

> **Leman's Law #21:**
> If he's young when you marry him,
> don't be surprised when he acts young.

A good marriage takes a *lot* of time. From my experience, it takes most couples at least ten years to break out of their families of origin and start building a new one. Lastborns have a way of acting like lastborns, even when their parents aren't around. It takes time to develop new roles, to adjust lifelong expectations, and to become familiar with your partner's rule book, the unspoken assumptions about how people should behave.

Even a sensitive husband doesn't "get it" sometimes. You're just as much a mystery to your husband as he is to you. He needs time to get to know how to live with a woman and how to read the nonverbal clues that you think are blatantly clear, but that he thinks are shrouded in mystery.

Take a common example from the workplace. A friend of mine, Gary Thomas, wrote in his book *Sacred Marriage* about how he learned that tears mean something very different to him from what they mean to his wife. Although he and Lisa had been married for more than twelve years, it wasn't until he read a personal experience piece written by a journalist with the *Washington Post* that he understood why his wife cried so much more frequently than he did. Gary writes:

> Liza Mundy was in an editorial meeting and became horrified when she found herself starting to cry. She was hot, bothered, and tired—nothing extraordinary, but it combined to make her want to cry. She writes,
>
> "Suddenly the heat had moved to my face and tears were springing to my eyes and I was blinking and blinking, hoping to drive them back. Only of course that was futile, because, as a friend later put it so beautifully, at this point in a crying-in-the-office experience, 'You're no longer crying because of what they're saying. You're crying because you're crying.' "
>
> Then, a paragraph or so later, Mundy wrote something that astonished me. "'Pay no attention to these tears; they are meaningless; I'm thinking quite clearly; this conversation isn't upsetting me nearly as much as it seems; I'm just fatigued and a little bit stressed

and feeling hot!' was what I wanted to say. Because I knew, like most women perhaps, that sometimes tears are no more significant than sweating."

As a man, I equate tears with weakness, with near-devastation. For me to cry in an office would take a major tragedy. And that's when I understood that perhaps tears mean something entirely different for me than they do for Lisa. I hear tears and think she's falling apart. She experiences tears and thinks she's merely sweating.[2]

Remind yourself again and again: A good marriage takes time. Fortunately, however, you can do some things to occasionally speed the process along.

What If I Married a Disrespectful Man?

If you have married a disrespectful man, does that mean you are forever condemned to live in a marriage devoid of respect?

Absolutely not. But to change the cycle, you'll need to change the way you've related to your husband in the past. To begin with, you'll need to develop a certain amount of self-respect because you'll be able to draw from that self-respect the strength to make a change in your marriage.

If you wait for your husband to change, nothing will happen. If you nag him, you'll become even more miserable than he is (and nagging will make him respect you less because nagging appears to be a weakness). So what can you do? The following advice applies to all men—those who respect their wives and those who don't.

A man is a creature of habit. To get a guy to notice something, you've got to break through his normal routine. Since he is naturally disposed to "fixing" things, sometimes he has to see for himself that something is broken before he pays attention to it.

For example, let's say Frank comes home from work one afternoon and immediately barks, "Where's my dry cleaning? Why didn't you pick up my dry cleaning?"

You know you can't win this argument, so refuse to get into it. If it really is your fault, apologize for your forgetfulness, then remind yourself that even if you did mess up, you deserve to be treated with respect. And tonight you're going to do something about it.

About an hour and a half later, Frank may notice that there's no dinner on the table. He'll probably scratch his head, go back into the den, and expect that you're just running a little late. But after another thirty minutes, when he doesn't hear anything happening in the kitchen, he's guaranteed to ask, "Where's dinner?"

Don't blow up. Don't whine. Say in a calm and casual voice, "I don't feel like cooking dinner."

"What do you mean you don't feel like cooking dinner?"

Stay cool. Don't get into an argument. Simply answer, "Well, Frank, you came home two hours ago, snapped at me, and said, 'Where's my dry cleaning?' The fact is, I spent most of the morning cleaning up after the *Monday Night Football* party you had with your friends, and then your mom called and asked me to come over this afternoon to run some errands for her. I'm sorry I forgot your dry cleaning, but I think I deserve to be treated with a little more respect. When you attack me without even trying to understand what my day was like, it makes me feel that you don't respect me. When I'm not respected, I don't feel like cooking."

Most often a husband doesn't *notice* when a wife feels demeaned. You have to do something to make him *see* that the relationship is broken. Words will fail 80 percent of the time. Create a *situation*, and the chances that your message will get through will increase dramatically.

The very things that frustrate you about your husband are frequently part of the package that comes with the opposite things that first attracted you. A woman may like the fact that a man isn't controlling, but then resent the fact that he lets others run over him. A woman may be thankful for her husband's strength; at the same time she is disappointed over his domineering nature. Knowing what you like will help you to endure what you don't like. Much of marital satisfaction comes down to focus. What will you keep thinking about: your husband's strengths or his weaknesses?

Focus on his weaknesses, and you'll find plenty to fret about. But let me urge you to give your husband a little more credit and a little more time.

A Man's Best Friend Is Not a Dog

My home church in Tucson asked me to speak at a steak fry. (Women might have coffees, but church marketing consultants have found that coffee beans aren't nearly as successful as meat at drawing men. If you want men to participate, promise them some meat!) More than 150 men showed up. They were committed Christians, by the way; for months they had attended a weekly Bible study that met at 6:00 A.M. Obviously their faith is very important to them, and discipline is not a problem in their lives if they're willing to get up that early to read and study God's Word.

I handed out a piece of paper to every man in attendance and asked each one to answer a single question: "How many times a day do you think about sex?"

The answer might surprise you. Remember, we're not talking about convicts, hedonists, or your average beer-guzzling, skirt-chasing

Joes. We're talking about guys who go to Promise Keepers events and most likely have well-worn Bibles.

The average number of times these committed Christian men thought about sex was *thirty-three times* a day. (Women, on average, think about sex once a day—and that's usually because their husbands bring it up!) Since men are awake about sixteen hours, they must think about sex about twice an hour. If your Christian husband is like most men and has been away at work about ten hours, he has had an average of twenty sexual thoughts since the last time you saw him.

Listen to me carefully, please: your husband is not a pervert for being seemingly obsessed with sex. There's nothing wrong with him for thinking that "once a day" should refer to more than vitamins. He's not sick for being turned on at 6:00 A.M. when he sees you coming out of the shower, naked, even though you've just had a tsunami of an argument. He's not a sex fiend. He's your normal, average, everyday man. And the sooner you become comfortable with your husband's desire for more and better sex, the sooner you'll be on your way to a happier marriage.

Leman's Law #22:

Your husband thinks about sex far more than you realize.

You need to know that your husband's interest in sex is not abnormal. Dr. Archibald Hart, who has counseled thousands of Christian men (many of them pastors and seminary professors) concerning their sexuality, writes, "Strong sexual feelings are common to all normal men. They are determined more by hormones than by evil desire. They are not sinful in and of themselves."[1]

Physiologically, the sex drive is determined largely by the level of testosterone in a man's body. Sexual desire in men is a hormone-driven urge that affects Christians and non-Christians, married and unmarried. It is a universal reality of living with a natural chemical that makes us men desire sex frequently.

Dr. Hart has found—as I have—that many Christian women who don't understand the male sex drive may label their husbands "sex-crazed maniacs" out of ignorance. They want their husbands to be masculine and normal in their desire to protect and provide. They don't want their husbands to act effeminate or to be weak and cowardly. But they want all that without the hormone-driven sex drive.

I'm sorry, but you can't have it both ways. If you want a normal husband, you're going to get one who thinks about sex a lot.

Inside the Mind of Christopher Christian

Physiologically, a man's favorite time to have sex is in the morning. A woman's favorite time to have sex is in June! Many women actually want more sex than their husbands do, but far more often it's the other way around, and these women usually don't understand what it's like living with testosterone running free inside their bodies. To give you an inside look, let's go behind the eyes of a mythical—but true-to-life—man we'll call "Christopher Christian."

Chris wakes up in the morning, and the first thing he notices is that Mr. Happy is especially pleased this day, waving at the world in full attention. Chris hasn't been awake for more than ten seconds, but the state of his body upon awakening means that his first thought is basically sexual. He might lean over and give his wife a quick, friendly squeeze, which will most likely be met with an "Umph, you've got to be kidding," or "Honey, the kids will wake up any minute!" or "Really, I haven't even brushed my teeth!"

Chris's wife responds this way because she has never lived with a Mr. Happy. She doesn't know what it's like to wake up with your blood flowing to one primary source of your body. She also doesn't realize that one quick, "Not on your life!" won't come close to putting Mr. Happy to sleep. No, Mr. Happy will remain happy for quite some time, whether the wife wants to think about that or not.

The real test comes thirty minutes later. Chris has read from his Bible and prayed for his family, then trudges upstairs to shave. He steps into the master bathroom, thinking about Paul's letter to the Galatians, when his wife steps out of the shower, smelling tantalizingly clean and looking as naked as she'll ever be.

Chris doesn't think, *Is this a good time to have sex? Let me see. I have to be at work in forty-five minutes, and Cheryl has to feed the kids breakfast soon so that they can get to school on time. No, this probably isn't a good time.* In an ideal world, maybe these somewhat mundane problems would prevail in Chris's mind, but this is the real world. Suddenly Chris thinks, *Naked wife! Let's have sex!*

Wife, how you handle Chris at this point is extremely important. While you may see his sudden interest as a nuisance at best and downright evil at worst, God made him in such a way that seeing you naked is likely to push every other thought straight out of his mind. He may well want to act irresponsibly.

Keep in mind: Chris now wants Cheryl for the second time in thirty-one minutes, but he is almost certain to be rebuffed again. Cheryl will throw a towel around herself, perhaps offer a grunt of disgust, and rush to put on her underwear, hoping that she can get downstairs before Chris reemerges from the bathroom. Chris will shave, shower, grab a quick cup of coffee, and drive to work.

If he lives near a large city, he will probably pass at least one billboard that contains a giant picture of a seductive woman whose legs are approximately fifteen feet long. She may be selling whiskey, a watch, suntan lotion, or dinner at Hooters, but she's been photographed and airbrushed to offer maximum allure, catching the male driver's sight. Teams of ad executives have pored over dozens of pictures to find the one angle, the one smile, and the one outfit that will positively, absolutely, make your husband look and want to look a second time.

A faithful Chris will look once and let it go at that. He'll tell Mr. Happy that now is not the time, and he may even pray or recite a Scripture. It's not yet 9:00 A.M., and Chris has already told his libido no three times.

At work Chris is surrounded by women who spent an average of sixty to ninety minutes making their faces look just right, choosing just the right scent, and finding the most flattering clothes to highlight the most flattering places. If he's in a position of power or working around a lonely, neglected woman, he may well be propositioned, indirectly or directly. Still, he says, "No."

Chris goes out with a few friends for lunch. A coworker has a sly grin on his face. "We thought we'd try a new place," he says, but Chris is immediately suspicious.

"What new place?"

"It's just a mile or so away."

"What's it called?"

"Don't you trust us, Chris?"

"What's it called?"

"The Playpen."

"You mean the strip bar?"

"Yeah."

"Sorry, not interested."

It's the fifth time Chris has denied his sex drive. He goes off to eat lunch by himself, opening up his local newspaper, only to discover that Victoria's Secret has purchased a full-page, full-color ad.

"Okay," he says quickly, "let's check out the sports pages."

That afternoon Chris returns to an office filled with women. Some, perhaps most, dress modestly and professionally, but a few wear low-cut blouses, short skirts, and perfume that makes him want to melt. They may have touched up their makeup during the lunch break, or maybe they paraded into the office in their spandex running shorts on the way to grabbing their clothes in their offices. Chris does his best to concentrate on his work and leave the office around 5:30.

When Chris comes home, he'll probably meet a legitimately tired wife. Because her day has been so packed, she probably has no idea how many or how varied have been the sexual temptations Chris has turned down, which is why she feels absolutely justified to tell him about ten o'clock, "We had sex three days ago, and you want it again? What's the matter with you? Are you some kind of sex nut?"

To help husbands sympathize with their pregnant wives, one organization developed a heavy pillow that men could wear around the waist. I think this is a great idea, just as I think it would be a great idea to have women live with a male libido for one week to see what it's like.

When you're a man, sexual desire is always there. Sometimes it's quieter than at other times, but it almost never goes away. Certainly after a pleasant time of consummation, the sexual urge will go to sleep for a short time, but it will inevitably wake up, much sooner than you would think, and once again pester the man who owns it until he experiences sex again.

Dr. Hart writes,

> Immediately after being sexually satisfied, the normal male may be able to focus elsewhere—for a while. But it is just a matter of time

> before his thoughts lead him back to sex. And I'm talking about the preacher as much as the truck driver.
>
> Sure, the average man thinks of other things, like football and politics, but eventually all mental roads lead back to this one central fixation: Sex. There are times when the obsession fades and even vanishes. Give him an intense challenge at work. Let him buy a new computer or sports car. Give him a golf bag or a fishing trip. He'll forget about sex for a while. But sooner or later, like a smoldering fire, it will flare up again. Strong, urgent, forceful, and impatient, the sex drive dominates the mind and body of every healthy male. Like it or not, that's the way it is.[2]

In case you're wondering whether this will ever change, Dr. Hart adds, "And I'm talking about men in their sixties, seventies, or even eighties, as well as about teenagers."[3]

Many Christian women may say, "That's all very well about men in *general*, but I thought *Christian* men are supposed to be different."

> **Leman's Law #23:**
> The sex drive is primarily a function of hormones, so Christian men don't desire sex any less than non-Christian men.

I've got news for you. They aren't. The expression of their sexuality may be different; the moral standards they live by and use to govern their sexuality will certainly be different; but the intensity of their sex drive won't be any different for one simple reason: hormones. Dr. Hart observes, "Why doesn't religion remove these sexual feelings? Because religious men have the same physical bodies as everyone else, and the sex drive is primarily a matter of hormones. Getting religious may help with control, but it clearly doesn't take sexual desire away."[4]

After decades of working with married couples, I've discovered that one of the greatest challenges facing marriage today is that women—Christian women in particular—do not understand the force of the male sex drive. And the few who do often don't care.

As a counselor, I'm now prepared to tell young women who are contemplating marriage, "If you're not willing right now to make a commitment to have sex at least two to three times a week for the rest of your life with this man, don't get married. If you do, you're committing fraud."

Allow me to soften this advice a bit. Of course, there are seasons when it would be cruel for a husband to make such frequent demands on his wife. When the wife is sick, for instance, in the later stages of pregnancy, or in the midst of a particularly difficult emotional time, the husband needs to learn how to show affection without expecting anything in return. And I honestly believe most men would be more than willing to suffer through such seasons if their wives made a more concerted effort the rest of the time.

It's still true that 95 percent of men get married assuming their wives will eagerly participate in regular sex. I'm one of those guys who "saved" himself until marriage. I bought into the bit about protecting my heart, avoiding diseases, and making sure I wasn't responsible for any out-of-wedlock pregnancies—all that stuff. Sande married a bona fide virgin.

But it came with a cost. My viewpoint was, *I've waited all these years, so now you're going to get everything I've got and then some.* As a young man, I couldn't imagine why a woman wouldn't want to have sex every day. Having been married for more than thirty-three years, I can give you a laundry list of reasons why a woman wouldn't want to have sex—starting with fatigue—but back then, I didn't have a clue.

I bet you don't have a clue either—particularly about how men are so attuned to sight. It's time for a reality check.

Reality Check

I love sports. I especially like to go to games at the stadium, eating hot dogs that have who knows what inside them (but taste just fine to me), where I can yell and scream and high-five my friend and not break any furniture. An experience there may help you understand what living in this world with an excess of testosterone is like for your husband. Because a man's sexual interest is primarily external and easily triggered by sight, even the most chaste husband will be enticed to look.

At a Buffalo Bills game with my favorite friend (a guy I affectionately call Moonhead), I noticed a young woman who was, shall we say, "put together." She was absolutely gorgeous, almost too good to be true. This young woman was standing within five inches of my seat!

I leaned over and said, "Moonhead, I just committed adultery."

He started to laugh, knowing exactly the person I was talking about, and I added, "Eight times!"

Moonhead laughed some more. The Bills completed one short play—an incomplete pass—after which I leaned over to Moonhead and said, "Nine."

I don't mean to make light of this. Obviously, I wasn't imagining sexual relations with this stranger; I wouldn't do that to my wife. But I want you to understand the thinking of men who are committed to our wives. Beauty turns our heads. I heard of a seminary professor—the kind of guy who spends five hours a day (or more) with his nose stuck in a textbook—who still confessed to his male students, "You get only one look, so you better make it a long one!"

These sight triggers come at us innocently all day long, but they are far from innocent. They are intense, and they can literally seize our attention, blocking out everything else. If I catch my wife bending over to put something in the dishwasher, for example, my thoughts can run wild. It doesn't matter whether she's wearing jeans, sweats, or a dress. The mere sight of her bending over can make the rest of the world melt away.

This phenomenon is doubly true when I'm looking at my wife, yet because I'm a man, I can't automatically "turn off" this response when I happen to glance at another woman. For example, I had a similar experience on an airplane. You don't have to come looking for me on an airplane. Being slightly claustrophobic, I always get the first seat in the first row. I need the space. I figure the airlines have hundreds of seats to negotiate. I practically subsidize them during the busy travel seasons, so they can accommodate me on this one item.

There I sat in 1B, an aisle seat, while the flight attendant waited on the person in 1C. I was looking straight ahead, then casually glanced over and noticed that the flight attendant was bending over to get something for the guy in 1C. I didn't choose the view. I did nothing to manipulate it, but there it was at eye level, and I can't say it displeased me. If I'm honest, I can't suggest that "Amazing Grace" was the first thing going through my mind.

Men are triggered by sight, and we live in a world where sexual images bombard us throughout the day. It wasn't always this way. One hundred years ago, the newspaper didn't contain photographs of real women wearing underwear. Some of the billboards today display pictures that would have made pornographers blush in earlier generations.

Because women frequently don't understand the impact that a low-cut blouse or a sexy perfume can have on a guy, they fail to understand what it feels like to literally be teased and provoked all day long, come home internally crying out for sexual release, and be rebuffed by a scoffing wife.

Added to all this, an even newer danger has arisen for men. Modern technology has made illicit sexual "entertainment" available within seconds, twenty-four hours a day. I have talked to wives who were devastated when they got a phone bill and found out their husbands had called a 1-900 sex line. The Internet has made pornography readily available to an entirely new generation of men. Though the Internet isn't as anonymous as people think it is, the man certainly no longer has to wear a baseball cap and a pair of sunglasses as he slyly walks into an adult store. All he has to do is boot up his computer and *voilà!* Pornography is there for the taking. The sense of shame and the fear of being caught that helped previous generations of men remain chaste no longer apply.

Just as dangerous are a growing number of Internet chat room affairs. Some people assume that because these cyber affairs are maintained on-line, they aren't really cheating. Such a view is very shortsighted. Marital fidelity isn't limited to actual bodily contact—it also includes emotional and verbal (even typewritten) intimacy. Besides, I'm seeing more and more cyber affairs become real-world affairs as the participants arrange to meet.

One man I know was out on a West Coast business trip that covered two cities: L.A. and Portland. In both hotels where he stayed, pornographic movies were just waiting to be ordered. The information left in the rooms made it clear that the movie's title wouldn't be included on the bill, so there would be no embarrassment. He went down to the lobby to get a snack and passed bins of skin magazines. Some of the travel literature in his room contained full-color ads for Gentlemen's Clubs, a euphemism for strip joints. *Throughout his entire trip, he was minutes or seconds away from illicit sexual entertainment.*

Fortunately, this man withstood the temptation. Even more fortunately, his wife was sympathetic and met him at the airport wearing a coat . . . and lingerie. As soon as my friend climbed into the car, his l up her coat just enough to give him a glimpse of what was) underneath and said, "I'm so glad you're back. I've really missed you." She rewarded his faithfulness and made it all the easier for him the next time he went on a trip.

But suppose his wife had said, "Sorry, Honey, I've had the kids all week and I'm just too tired." Or maybe she was a little more accommodating, but still demeaning: "I guess so if you really need it. Get a towel, and let's get this over with so I can get some sleep." The wife's response will have a major impact on how well that man is able to handle the temptations the next time he hits the road.

Wife, in the twenty-first century, sexual disinterest on your part is flat out dangerous. Maybe in the Garden of Eden, where sexual images didn't abound, sexual apathy could be managed. But this isn't the Garden of Eden, and your husband isn't living in a pure world. *If you want him to be faithful, the least you can do is never give him a reason to look elsewhere.*

To make sure you get this straight, I want to give you ten additional reasons why your husband frequently thinks about sex. What you choose to do with this information is up to you, but I want to make sure you know exactly what is going on in your husband's mind (and other places).

Ten Reasons Your Husband Is Always Thinking About Sex

Because so many women have asked me to explain *why* men seem obsessed about sex, I'm going to attempt to list the reasons. You may not like them, but at least you'll be able to better understand what's going on inside your husband.

1. He needs to feel needed.

It is very emotionally fulfilling for a man to have a wife who is interested in him sexually. A man is external. If you want a man to feel wanted and needed, words won't cut it; you need to pursue him sexually. Your husband won't care what you say with your mouth if the rest of your body is screaming out, "Don't touch me!"

2. He needs the physiological release.

Remember, sexual desire is largely a matter of hormones. The level of testosterone varies from man to man. You may have a twenty-four-hour husband, a forty-eight-hour husband, or a once-every-five-days husband, but every man has a clock that is counting the minutes until the next sexual release. Eventually he is going to feel that he *needs* a sexual experience. I can't overstress this point, in large part because your body is so different. For a man, sexual desire is physically based and ever present.

3. He feels more insecure and less desirable as he grows older.

We'll talk about this in a little more depth later on, but for now, realize that when a wife maintains an enthusiastic sexual interest in her husband, she gives him a tremendous gift as he faces the debilitating effects of thinning hair and a bulging waistline.

4. He feels close to you through your sexual relationship.

You may be most thankful you married your husband when you watch him play with the children or help out around the house. Perhaps you appreciate his ability to bring home paychecks or to make you feel safer when he's home. Maybe you feel closest to him when you cuddle up next to him in bed. Your husband probably feels closest to you when you're having sex. That's what makes him say,

"I'm so glad I married this woman." If you want your husband to utter these words, you have to meet him where it matters most—to *him*.

5. He is a physical being.

Many men solve problems through sex; it all goes back to their being physical beings. Women tend to be more emotional and want to talk things out. But from a man's perspective, the problem is solved when the two of you have sex. Just look at how two guys can get into a vicious fistfight, shake hands, and then act like best friends. Once they've had it out, the problem is over.

6. It's his only real fun.

Men work hard today, then they come home and try to be involved parents. Honoring all of their commitments requires sacrifice and self-denial. Sex is the one thing that's free and really fun. So many men get battered at the office that they feel as if they're being used, abused, and challenged all day long. Watching television provides an escape, but it rarely provides true recreation. It's far more like a mind-numbing drug.

For sheer fun, nothing beats a romp under the covers. If you don't want your husband to spend all his free time on the golf course or out on the town, show him a different way to exercise.

7. *Sight turns him on, and there are sights everywhere he goes.*

"Made you look!"

Yeah, it sure did. The huge billboard publicizing a restaurant chain was covered with eight very well-endowed women, all wearing tight T-shirts. The headline "Made you look!" showed that the ad company understands men. It's very difficult for us men *not* to look.

Consider King David, whom the Bible describes as a "man after

God's own heart." Yet he was completely overcome by the sight of Bathsheba bathing and decided he *had* to have her, even though she was married to another man.

After committing adultery and murder, the man after God's own heart found himself in a heap of trouble, and it all began with sight. Your husband is being sexually provoked all day long. He can't help this—and he needs your help to find a chaste outlet.

8. Sex provides great release from stress.

When a husband and a wife are naked together in bed, it doesn't really matter to the husband whether he's in a Marriott or a Motel 6. He doesn't care whether he likes his job or whether his business will succeed. For a few glorious minutes, he is transported out of a competitive world and set free to enjoy physical intimacy with his wife. When he finally climaxes, he will have a very pleasant sense of satisfaction and peace. Poets used to use the metaphor of dying to describe a man's orgasm because that's almost what it feels like. His body is spent, and he's able to slip into a comforting afterglow of unparalleled relaxation.

9. It may be the most spiritual thing he ever does.

The notion of two people becoming one is a profoundly spiritual truth. As a Christian, I believe the sex act has as much to say about what happens within our souls as it does with what goes on inside our bodies. A husband and a wife create a holy union marked by a distinctly spiritual element. A man may have difficulty with contemplative prayer, but this is a spirituality he can truly enjoy!

10. He is one-dimensional.

Women, as a rule, are more divested in other people—their children, their girlfriends, their mothers, you name it. Men tend to have fewer friends and therefore need a more intense relationship with their wives. If they're not getting the intimacy they desire from their spouses, it's far less likely that they have a guy friend they can talk to. Therefore, when men are consistently rebuffed by their wives, they're likely to turn to other women.

Now that we've covered the basic nature of a man's sexual desire, I want to throw in an additional element. It is so important that it deserves an entire chapter of its own. In spite of what you've just read, you've misunderstood me if you think your husband's greatest need is sex. It's not.

Read the next chapter to find out what it is.

10

Sexual Fulfillment

"Doctor, I gotta tell you; I think I could have sex with my husband twice a day and it *still* wouldn't be enough. I *want* to please him, I really do. I just don't think it's possible!"

"Alice" came to me confused about the quantity of sex she suspected her husband wanted to experience. One hour later, she left my office thinking not about quantity, but about *quality*.

Everything I talked about in the previous chapter could possibly mislead you. I'm *not* simply saying, "You need to have sex with your husband more often." Your husband's greatest need in marriage isn't to have more sex. Nor is it more money, better-tasting food, or more respect. Your husband truly desires sexual *fulfillment*.

That men typically want more sex isn't much of a secret. *Why* men want more sex often is. A lot of women feel the way Alice does: "No matter how much sex I give my husband, he'll want more!" But if you talk to the husband, he'll likely respond, "If the *quality* of my sex life was better, and I had a wife who occasionally initiated sex so I didn't always have to bring it up, and who was more assertive and aggressive when we did have sex, I think I'd need it much less. I just want to know that she really wants me."

That last line—"I just want to know that she really wants me"—is the key to understanding male sexual desire. Let me bring you in on a little male secret: the biggest sexual turn-on for healthy men is the emotional one. There's nothing like seeing your wife thoroughly enjoying herself in the midst of sexual relations. Realizing that you can bring your wife pleasure—even ecstasy—is tremendously fulfilling emotionally. It makes you feel like a man.

That's why I think God knew what He was doing when He made women the way they are. Many men have told me they sometimes get jealous of their wives' orgasms. Because of the way you ladies are built, you can be at a sexual peak seemingly forever. Some wives can practically wake up the man on the moon if they're experiencing a good orgasm, while we men are forced to content ourselves with about six seconds of pleasure. Granted, they are pleasurable seconds.

> **Leman's Law #24:**
>
> Men don't just crave the physical release in sex. They hunger for the emotional fulfillment that comes from pleasing their wives sexually.

Since men are physical beings, it shouldn't be a surprise that we express our fulfillment physically.

All of this explains my emphasis on a man's wanting sexual *fulfill-*

ment, not just sex. There's a major difference between the two. A "willing" wife tells her husband, "All right, Honey, go ahead, but please pull my nightie down when you're finished. And let's hurry it up. The kids might wake up." An "eager" wife shows her sexual hunger and enjoyment. A man will choose the latter every time. He would probably choose having sex with an eager wife once a week over having sex with a merely willing wife once a day.

Part of this comes down to the male ego, which we'll discuss in more detail later in this book. If you want to rob a man of his masculinity, if you want to cut him off at his knees, here's how you do it: regularly adopt this "okay, let's just get it over with" approach to sex. (It's also a great way to drive a man into another woman's arms.)

> **Leman's Law #25:**
>
> Sexual fulfillment for a man requires far more than a willing wife. It requires an aggressive, eager, and fully engaged wife.

And that's why sexual fulfillment is a key to a happy marriage. The truth is, a man wants to be held, even cuddled. What often happens, however, is that when a wife slips into bed and gets the least bit cuddly, innocently saying, "It's so nice to sleep next to a warm body," hardly ten seconds go by before her nightie is wrapped around her ankles and she's staring up at the ceiling thinking, *This isn't what I had in mind!* The natural result is that she stops cuddling and stops pursuing her husband, which makes *him* more grabby, which makes *her* initiate even less, and so on and so on.

If your man is getting the kind and quantity of sex that he wants, to cuddle and meet your needs for affection without flip- your back and pinning you to the mattress. Don't buy into the lie that men are buffoons who don't have feelings. While the popular consensus says that men aren't sensitive, the truth is, men are *very* sensitive. The catch is that we're sensitive only when we feel safe and when our sexual needs are met.

By the way, while all of what I'm saying might sound as if I'm serving only the man's interest, there are many ways in which *you* will benefit from being married to a sexually fulfilled husband.

Why You Want a Sexually Fulfilled Husband

A sobering moment in the process of writing this book came after I talked to several women about what they wanted to know about men. I asked one in particular, "If women really understood how important sexual fulfillment is for a man, would they change and make a greater effort to help provide it?"

There was a long pause. She sighed and said, "No, probably not."

Why should you care about your husband's sex drive? I can give you a big reason for caring: your husband's continued fidelity. Dr. Hart's research confirms what I have found true in my practice:

> By being able to accept their spouse's strong urges, [wives] will build the greatest protection possible against sexual failure in their own marriage. I have yet to meet a wife—accepting and nonjudgmental toward her spouse's sexuality, sharing open sexual communication with him—who had to contend with a wayward husband. Total openness in the arena of sexuality is the best protection I know against adultery.[1]

I realize that you may not be able to imagine being assertive and aggressive in your sexual relationship with your husband. It's not your nature. Or you may lack the energy. All wives experience this struggle from time to time. Not that long ago, I looked seductively at my wife and said, "You want to be the wife of a happy husband?"

"No!" she said, knowing exactly what I meant. "I've got work to do! I've got to pick up the kids, send out the Christmas cards, go shopping for dinner, and pick up the dry cleaning! I don't have *time* to make a happy husband!"

When you find yourself buried in life's demands, when you know you've slipped a little in meeting your husband's sexual needs, remind yourself of the following truths.

A Frustrated Husband Eventually Becomes an Angry Husband

I wish you could sit in my counselor's chair for a week and hear the utter frustration—usually turning to anger—as men talk about how their wives use their husbands' sex drive as a tool to manipulate and demean them. I realize every marriage is different. Sometimes the wife is more interested in sex than the man is, but one thing usually stays the same: *whoever wants the least sex probably has the most power in bed.*

That makes sense, doesn't it? If a Christian man knows that there is only one place biblically where his sexual needs can be met, and the wife knows that she is the "keeper of the key," so to speak, who do you think has the power in that situation?

When a man is made to beg, when a man is told he is a "sex fiend," when a man is merely accommodated rather than wanted by his wife, it is only a matter of time until the marriage suffers severe icing over.

Wife, you have to understand that a man can't completely turn off his sex drive. You think he *likes* the pressure it puts him under? It's a physical thing, driven by hormones, not a spiritual disease. If you use his natural desire against him, if he senses that you are grasping for control rather than serving him, he will resent you, even when you say yes. He will slowly become bitter and angry, falling ever deeper into a smoldering stew of discontentment.

He will probably take what you give him, but he'll never forget the way it was given—and he'll resent you for it. He'll remember that you took advantage of him, and the next time you ask him for a favor, don't be surprised that he is slow to respond.

Scripture Tells You to Accommodate Your Husband

Can anybody deny that the apostle Paul was a great saint? I mean, look at all the churches and schools that are named after him! The guy must have been pretty holy, right? Sure, he was. That makes what he wrote in 1 Corinthians even more interesting:

> Let the husband render to his wife the affection due her, and likewise also the wife to her husband. The wife does not have authority over her own body, but the husband does. And likewise the husband does not have authority over his own body, but the wife does. Do not deprive one another except with consent for a time, that you may give yourselves to fasting and prayer; and come together again so that Satan does not tempt you because of your lack of self-control. (1 Cor. 7:3–5)

It doesn't take a Bible scholar to figure out what Paul was saying (Paul was my kind of saint!). "Affection" clearly refers to conjugal rights, that is, sexual intercourse. The Leman translation goes like this: "Paul said to married couples, 'Do it. If you want to stop for prayer, that's okay, but when you're finished praying, come back and do it again.'" That's Scripture.

Previous generations of Christians talked about "the marriage debt." Francis de Sales, a well-known Christian writer in the sixteenth century, put 1 Timothy 5:8 together with 1 Corinthians 7:3–5 to say, "If a person does miracles while in the state of marriage, but does not render the debt of marriage to his spouse or does not concern himself with his children, 'he is worse than an infidel.'"[2]

This celibate man taught married women that sexual interest is a "debt" they incur when they enter marriage (this is true for both partners, of course). Just as husbands are obligated to be faithful, to provide for and protect the family, so wives have an obligation to meet the sexual needs of their husbands (and vice versa). To enter marriage and then withhold this element is an act of fraud. De Sales would say that your spiritual life is a sham if you are denying your husband. Do all the miracles you want, but if you withhold sex, you are "worse than an infidel."

A Sexually Fulfilled Man Is a More Helpful Husband

Sex is one of the ways a man loves his wife. Just as you think it's pretty important for a man to be affectionate and helpful around the house, so the man thinks it's vital for you to be eager and even aggressive in bed.

But here's the payoff. Often a man will say, "Once I feel secure that you really love me and want to be with me sexually, then I can do all kinds of things to help you. I can be a better father; I can help out with dishes; I'll want to be at home on time."

If your husband is sexually fulfilled, he'll want to please you. He'll have a sense of pride about meeting your needs. Home will become the focus of his life. When the sexual need isn't met, however, a man has a tendency to become angry, sullen, withdrawn, childlike, aggressive, and mean-spirited.

Look at it this way: your actions in bed will go a long way in determining your husband's attitude in the other rooms of the house. I'm not saying his poor attitudes are your fault, but I am saying that you can positively influence those attitudes over time.

Your Husband's Faithfulness Deserves Your Appreciation

If your husband has a strong sex drive and expresses it by wanting to have sex with you four or five times a week, at least be thankful that he is pursuing *you* and not an illicit sex life. In my line of work, I come across a lot of guys who spew their sexual energy into Internet porn, X-rated movies, pornographic magazines, strip clubs, or frequent masturbation. Hani Miletski, a certified sex therapist who has many clients in the legal profession, says she is seeing a growing number of professional men in the Washington, D.C., area turn to their computers instead of their wives in pursuit of sexual excitement.[3]

It's sad, but true. More and more men are creating a sex life apart from their wives. They don't connect their sexuality with their wives because their wives aren't their primary sexual partners. Consequently, true intimacy in marriage is always going to be a problem. Loyalty won't mean much either.

Sure, you may grow weary trying to meet your husband's sexual desires, but remember this: *faithful men usually desire sex with their wives more frequently than unfaithful men do.* A man who shows no sexual interest in his wife might as well be waving a red flag at me. If there are no sexual orientation issues, I'm going to suspect that the hubby is building a little sexual hobby on the side, either satisfying himself or going to someone else for sexual satisfaction.

In this sense, wives should be thankful when their husbands turn their sexual desires *on them.* I've walked many women through the angst of marital unfaithfulness—whether with a real person or a fantasy image—and the feelings of betrayal are devastating and extremely painful. You don't want to experience this, believe me. Most women have no idea how common illicit sexual activity is among men, but I think one statistic will help you realize how big sexual entertainment has become today: add up all the money that our country spends on Broadway productions and regional and non-profit theaters, throw in the total revenues for every opera, ballet, jazz, and classical music performance in this country, and then pool all that money. You'll still have less money than the revenues earned by strip clubs *alone*.[4]

Men have an enormous sexual appetite, and many of them choose to meet that hunger outside the home. If your husband prefers you, be thankful.

With all of these thoughts in mind, are you willing to put a little more effort into pleasing your husband sexually? If you are, get ready—we're going to be very specific!

Why Men Like Variety in Sex

One of the main reasons that a man seems to want so much sex is that he rarely experiences the kind he truly desires, the kind that touches his soul and makes him sigh, "I'm married to the most wonderful woman on the face of the earth." The typical man who shows up in my office resembles a hungry person who needs to snack constantly because he never gets a feast that finally satisfies him.

Allow me to use a word picture to clarify what I mean. Have you ever asked your husband to hold you, only to have him bring along the sports pages and put a hand on your knee while he reads the paper? You and I both know that's not holding. You do the same thing to your husband, however, when you are merely *tolerant* of sex and obviously not involved. Tolerant sex to a man is not really sex. It won't begin to touch his deepest emotional needs.

"That's fine, Dr. Leman, but what do I do when I'm genuinely tired?"

Because it's likely that your sex drive will be less intense than your husband's, you may need to learn how to give your husband the gift of sexual variety without having to fully involve yourself. Can I let you in on a little secret? Sometimes if you really are too tired to have sexual intercourse, there's something even more pleasurable to a man. No, I'm not talking about oral sex; I'm talking about what schoolboys refer to as "hand jobs." For most men, there's nothing more pleasurable. You can put a smile on your husband's face without too much effort on your part, and he'll go to sleep thinking, *I must be the luckiest man who ever lived. I'm so glad I married this woman.*

It comes down to this: Do you really want to please your mate? If you do, you're going to have to initiate more variety in your lovemaking. In addition to an occasional hand job, and beyond trying out different positions, you can vary the time and place. Long, slow, luxuriant sex is wonderful, but there's also a place for intense, fun "quickies." It is not unusual for a man to wake up in the morning with an erection. He has a warm wife sleeping next to him, but he has learned from previous refusals not to touch his mate before she has her shower or brushes her teeth. You know what? There are times when a man could care less—in fact, he might enjoy sex more—when you are unshowered. He wants the intensity of the moment; he wants *spontaneity*.

Talk about sex! I think it's healthy for each spouse to occasionally ask, "Honey, what are three things I can do in our sex life that would make you feel special?" You might be surprised by your husband's response. He might say, "Come to bed fully clothed." Why? Because some men really enjoy undressing their wives.

Couples could save themselves a fortune by talking to each other before they visit a therapist. Did you hear of the wife who always bought her husband 7 Up when she went to the grocery store? Ten years after they were married, her husband went shopping and brought home root beer.

"What, no 7 Up?" the wife asked. "I thought that was your favorite."

"Honey, I *hate* 7 Up. The only reason I drink it is that's all we've ever had around the house!"

The same miscommunication happens with sexual relations. You can't expect to get married and immediately know all there is to know about pleasing your mate sexually. Marital sex is more like on-the-job training—but it's fun work if you can get it!

Just to prime the pump, here are some ideas to add spice and variety to your sex life. Notice that all of them show your initiation. Remember, this aspect of initiation is just as important to your husband as is the physical act that will follow.

- Wear your spiked heels to bed—with nothing else.
- The next time you're at a restaurant, casually lean over and tell him you're not wearing any underwear.
- The next time you pack hubby's lunch, include a bag of green M & M's (or stuff a baggie of them into his briefcase) to communicate that you are thinking about your next sexual encounter with him.
- Buy one of those temporary tattoos, and tell him he'll have to strip-search you to find it.
- "Borrow" his Bible (without his knowledge), and put Post-it

Notes in the Song of Songs, with his name on the relevant passages.

- The next time you come to bed, use an extra two squirts of his favorite perfume.
- Suggest a round of strip poker.
- Occasionally flash your husband (at home) in a teasing manner.
- Whisper to your husband that tonight you're so interested, you'll do *anything* he wants.

While you work to add variety to your sexual relationship, you also need to be careful about unintentionally undercutting this with acts that are extremely frustrating to many men. Let's talk about some of the things that frustrate men the most.

How to Create a Sexually Frustrated Husband

I was sitting in church with my family when the pastor read a passage from the book of Proverbs: "Hope deferred makes the heart sick" (Prov. 13:12). These words are so true. Wherever your husband's hope is deferred, at that point a sickness starts creeping into his heart—and your marriage. We can exist with deferred hopes for only so long until they eventually poison us and wreak havoc on our souls and relationships.

Some women don't have a clue about *how* they are frustrating their husbands. In that spirit, I'm going to show you how to create a sexually frustrated man. (The goal, of course, is not to do that!)

Surefire Ways to Make Your Husband Miserable

1. String him along.

Every time your husband hints about sex, lead him on. Tell him, "Maybe tonight," knowing full well that there's a higher chance of Pluto crashing into Earth than there is of any sexual intimacy happening under your covers. Keep doing this on a regular basis, and you'll get your wish—an enormously frustrated, bitter, and angry husband.

2. Act like a martyr.

Give in, but make sure your husband knows you're doing it grudgingly. Don't let there be any hint that you might have the slightest interest or pleasure in sleeping with him. Make sure he knows that you're doing him a favor and that he'll "owe" you for it big time.

3. Accuse him of being a sex maniac.

Make sure he never forgets that you harbor suspicions he may be a sex fiend, a pervert, and a seriously disgusting man who is completely abnormal for wanting to have frequent sex with his wife. If he's a Christian, make sure he knows you think he's a carnal one for harboring thoughts about the two of you having sex.

4. Use sex as a weapon.

Punish your husband by denying him sexual relations. Every time he breaks one of your rules or forgets to pick up a gallon of milk on the way home, make sure he pays for it in bed. If you've had a disagreement, insist that at least five days, a dozen roses, and ten apologies pass your way before you'll let him touch you.

5. Talk to others about your husband's sex life.

Pour out your frustration over your husband's ravenous (or nonexistent) sex drive. Laugh about his particular foibles. Maybe he's too fast; maybe he's too slow; maybe he's too shy. It doesn't really matter *what* you talk about as long as you open up your husband's most intimate secrets to someone. If you really want to get him, tell his secrets to his family—his brothers or sisters or mother. If you want to be creative, ask them to "pray" about his sex life; that'll cover your back in case any smug Christian accuses you of gossip.

6. Don't try to meet his requests.

Wait until your husband finally gets up the courage to tell you he thinks you would be really sexy in a leopard-skin teddy or bodysuit. Pause a moment, laugh in his face, and never consider trying one on. Dismiss all his ideas to introduce creativity into your love life as ridiculous, weird, or just plain hilarious. Keep doing this until he knows he can't ever share the deepest desires of his heart with you.

7. Stay silent.

Don't give your husband a hint that you like what he's doing. If you do say something, make sure it's G rated. *Never* directly refer to body parts—either yours or his—and do your best to muffle all sounds, verbal and nonverbal.

8. Judge his performance.

Make sure your husband knows that on his best day, you'd give him only a C+ in bed. (I hope this doesn't apply to you, but if you really want to be demeaning, compare him to previous lovers and point out how terrible he is.) Laugh at his attempts to try something new. When he's feeling vulnerable, make a joke about something he did in bed or laugh about a fantasy he shared.

9. Make him jump through hoops.

"Okay, Howard, we can make love, but first you need to take out the garbage, fix the leaky faucet, take a shower, shave, brush and floss your teeth, trim your toenails, bring in a towel for me to lie on, turn off all the lights, and get it all done by ten o'clock because I have an early morning meeting tomorrow." Show him that sex is about 180 on your list of priorities. That'll really make him feel small.

I certainly hope that you are committed to avoiding any of the errors I've discussed. One of the best ways to do this, however, is to focus on the positive. Let's consider how you can become the wife of a sexually fulfilled husband.

How to Create a Sexually Fulfilled Husband

"Oh, that makes me frisky," I told Sande.

She laughed. "What *doesn't* make you feel frisky?"

I asked a woman who had been married about fifteen years what she would tell a twenty-year-old engaged woman on the day before her wedding. "I would focus on the whole sex thing," she said, "because it has been such a huge issue in our marriage. If I knew this girl to be anything like me, that is, ultranaive, I'd want to prepare her. Right before I got married, somebody threw me for a loop when she said that sex wasn't important. I maintained that misunderstanding for some time, and it really affected my marriage.

"Three years into my marriage, I started thinking that maybe there was something wrong with my husband—that he was oversexed or something—so I doubted his relationship with the Lord and my ability to give him what he wanted or needed. I've since learned, however, that the problem wasn't with my husband, but with my understanding of men and their needs. I now understand how important sex is to my husband, without viewing that as some animalistic thing."

I couldn't have said it better myself. The woman who really "gets it" is the woman who understands the difference between sex and sexual fulfillment. As I said before, you could give your husband sex every night of the year, but that wouldn't be enough if you merely made yourself available. The emotional aspect of sex charges a man through occupational hassles, taxes, and the general humdrum of life.

Here are a few suggestions if you want to be the wife of a sexually fulfilled husband.

1. Talk about what ***you*** *want.*

If a wife leaves a note in her husband's briefcase that says, "I'd really like us to 'get together' tonight, and I'd like to do it in front of a fire," I guarantee you, that man will get firewood, even if he has to cut down the endangered-species tree in front of the city museum! The thought that a wife is imagining a situation in which she would enjoy sex is a real turn-on you can give your husband. I keep trying to tell women: most thoughtful men *want* to please their wives, *especially* in bed. Give your husband a chance to do that.

2. Become comfortable with sound.

Silence is *not* golden, at least not in bed. Think about this: some estimates suggest that phone sex is now a *billion-dollar* industry. Some men are so starved for sound that they will pay three to five dollars *a minute* to hear a woman talk dirty to them. I'll be the first to say that pornography is a sick, destructive industry, but as a psychologist, I realize that many men are frustrated with overly reserved wives. I'm not in any way suggesting women should talk like X-rated porn stars if they don't feel comfortable with doing that. On the other hand, if you can handle it and your husband desires it, you might venture into the R-rated category now and then.

I know this isn't easy. Many women have sat in my office, horrified at the words and expressions their husbands have asked them to use. But maybe you can wade into this. Without getting explicit, you can certainly learn to use common words creatively: *harder* and *deeper* are two that come to mind. Sprinkle these words in the appropriate context, and you'll have a happier husband.

Sound goes beyond words, of course. Let your husband *hear* your pleasure. If you know it's pleasing him, there's nothing wrong with adding a little volume. After all, you touch him in certain ways just to excite him, don't you? Well, then, why can't you excite him by deliberately using your voice?

3. Enjoy sex.

Women are equipped physiologically to enjoy sex even more than men are. We're talking potential here. A woman needs a sensitive lover to experience this type of pleasure. Because of this, you may need to teach your husband what pleases you. You'll have to be extremely sensitive and creative so he doesn't interpret this as criticism. Try something like this, which sounds enticing more than critical: "You know what would *really* turn me on? Having you touch me like this. . . ."

If your husband gets lucky and does something that feels particularly nice, shout out your approval! Make sure he knows exactly how much you enjoy that. Just because he's a man (even if he had prior sexual experience) doesn't mean he understands your body. He needs your help. Every woman's body is different, and it's your job to help your husband understand how your particular body responds.

The point is that by learning to thoroughly enjoy sex, you're going to help your husband enjoy his sexual experience even more. Revel in the pleasure, which is there by God's design. Delight in the way He created your body to receive such prolonged enjoyment. When you feel the ecstasy coming over you, let your husband know how much pleasure he's bringing you. And after you've been satisfied, *thank him*. Boy, you'll really make him feel ten feet tall if you sincerely thank him for giving you pleasure.

4. Shock him.

One young wife casually told her husband, "I got a haircut today."

He looked at her, shrugged his shoulders, and said, "I'm sorry, Honey, but I didn't notice."

"Of course not," she said coyly. "I'm not talking about my head. I'd like to show it to you later tonight, after the kids are in bed."

Let me tell you, that husband was about as charged as a husband could get. His wife finally put her foot down when he tried to get the kids into their pajamas at 6:45!

Do you know *why* he was so sexually charged? His wife did something that surprised him *and* that showed an interest in him. A woman usually gets a haircut so that she looks good to everybody, but this "haircut" was solely for her husband. She immediately created a feeling of intimacy and a shared secret. Suddenly her husband felt especially close to her.

Doing this type of thing creates sexual fulfillment: shared intimacy, exclusively between the two of you. If you want your husband to appreciate you and to feel close to you, this is how you do it.

5. *Make work fun.*

Does your husband have a private office at work? Maybe going all the way would be too risky, but can you show up at his office in a long coat and surreptitiously flash him? Maybe you can leave a piece of personal clothing in his briefcase with a note that reads: "Normally I'd be wearing these today, but I've decided to go without them, since as soon as you get home they're going to come off anyway." Sign the card with a lipstick smooch, and expect hubby to come home early.

I know a woman who worked as an assistant for her husband, who happened to be a doctor. One time, while hubby was meeting with a patient, she walked in and said, "Can I see you for a moment, Doctor?"

"Excuse me," the doctor said.

As soon as she got him in a side room, she went to work. It didn't take long. The doctor washed up and returned to his patient. While the person being examined had to spend a few minutes leafing through a magazine, that doctor certainly came out a much happier and fulfilled man—and probably a better doctor to boot!

Work provides opportunities for special greetings when hubby gets home. I know a couple who live out in the country. One night the husband had to work late; he was under a lot of stress, but finally called around eight o'clock, saying he was on his way home. The wife stripped bare, put on a coat, and walked out beside the deserted road near their house. As soon as she saw her husband's headlights, she dropped the coat and became the world's sexiest hitchhiker!

Her husband practically cried later on as they finished up in bed. "You know, Honey," he said, "that's the first time in about six weeks I've been able to forget about work."

6. Kidnap him.

Take your husband out to dinner, wear your sexiest dress, and casually drop your hand underneath the tablecloth, occasionally rubbing his thigh. About the time he's ready to order dessert, slide a hotel key his way and watch his eyes pop out.

Make advance reservations at a place with a hot tub, or take him on a walk to a remote meadow until you "accidentally" stumble upon a blanket nicely laid out, just waiting for you. A little advance planning will go a very long way. (Keep in mind, this is risky unless you're very familiar with the area. I don't want to get anybody arrested!)

A not-so-young wife packed a backpack for a day hike. The kids had moved out of the house, the husband felt as if he was being put on a shelf at work, and the wife figured he could use a pick-me-up. The husband never thought to look inside the backpack as his wife handed it over; he dutifully put it on as the two seemingly meandered through the woods. When they come across a secluded clearing and his wife started undressing him, he didn't know what to think—until she told him to open the backpack and he saw a blanket, a tube of KY Jelly, and a Polaroid camera. The realization that his wife had *planned* an outdoor sexual experience just about put him over the top.

7. *Beat him to the punch.*

Since men are always complaining about not getting enough sex, why not put this argument to rest? *You* be the one to initiate relations two days in a row! Since I speak a lot, I receive all kinds of anecdotes and articles. One person sent me an article from a national women's magazine describing how a woman decided to have sex seven days in a row with her husband. She found it quite helpful and enjoyable as it shook them out of their rut and taught them to look for new things.

Obviously you can't keep this up forever, but if you take the lead on a semiregular basis, at least you'll stop the complaining. Being the initiator can be a matter of self-defense.

A woman came to me for counseling because her husband wanted sex *all* the time. She was exhausted and wondered how long she could last.

I listened to her for a while and had a pretty good hunch about what was going on, so I asked her, "You want to turn the tables here?"

"What do you mean?" she asked.

"Why don't you start pursuing *him?*"

She had every right to get up and leave the room immediately. After all, she was complaining about her husband wanting too much sex, and I was telling her to initiate even more sex. But she heard me out.

"I mean it," I said. "Why don't you try waking him up in the middle of the night or surprising him as soon as he gets home?"

I had a suspicion here, and as it turned out, I was right. The woman took my suggestion to heart and within days her husband experienced impotence. The underlying issue wasn't just sex; it was control. She didn't want an impotent husband, either, of course, but at least now the real issues could be addressed.

In a healthy situation, however, pursuing your husband sexually beyond your typical pattern will be received as a welcome gift. For example, let's say the two of you go to a hotel on a Friday night and make mad, passionate love. On Saturday morning, wake him up, rub his chest, and say, "Will you do me a favor today?"

He'll probably grunt, "What?" assuming that you're going to ask him to go shopping.

Instead, say, "Make love to me again, and this time give me everything you've got."

These little extras mean a lot to a man. People who study these things tell me that you don't really start burning fat until after you've exercised about thirty minutes. If you can exercise a bit longer than that, they say, you'll get the maximum benefit. In the same way, if you can go just beyond your typical pattern sexually, doing just a little extra, the impact will feel gigantically larger to your husband. That's where love is really shown and where love is gratefully received.

8. Change your persona.

I'm frequently asked, "How can we keep sex fresh and fun?" Here's an exercise that any woman can carry out.

The next time your husband comes home, meet him at the door and pull him inside, closing the door. Start unbuckling his belt buckle. You might think you should start with the shirt or the coat, but trust me on this one. Go for the belt. You touch that buckle first, and you've got his full and undivided attention.

He's going to say something. Put your forefinger on his lips, physically (but not verbally) telling him to be quiet. Let the only sounds be sounds of passion. Don't say anything yourself. Just open up his pants.

Remember, *don't say anything*. If he tries to talk, don't answer. Just let your hands do the conversing.

What's happening here psychologically is that you're becoming a mystery woman. Since you're behaving out of character, he's going to feel that this is an entirely new situation—in a good way. He's not sure what's going on.

Men love it.

You may be thinking, *But what do I do when his pants are opened up?*

Don't talk, stay silent, and keep focused and intent on getting him naked. You'll both figure out what to do next.

Or you may be thinking, *Dr. Leman, you're assuming that my husband is crazy about sex and that I'm totally uninterested. In our marriage, it's exactly the opposite.* Don't worry. I haven't forgotten you—I've talked to many wives who are in your situation. Let's turn our attention to what a wife can do when her husband is the one who seems uninterested in sex. You need to know what's going on inside your husband's mind.

What If You Want Sex, but He Doesn't?

There's an elementary school near where I live. Every day, a stunningly beautiful young mother drops her two daughters off. She gets out of the car, bends over to kiss and hug them, and then gets back into her car. Traffic stops, and it's amazing how some of the male staff always seem to be walking by at just the right time! This mother is certainly attractive enough to tempt many a man to alter his schedule.

The men who are staring don't know that the woman's husband can hardly stand to touch her. He couldn't have a more beautiful wife, but he has almost no sexual interest in her.

I tell this true story to encourage you as you wonder whether something is wrong with you. You've read all that I've written, and you think, *I wish my husband wanted sex more often, but every time I bring it up he's not interested!*

What causes a man to be uninterested in sex?

1. Impotence

Few things make a man feel as ashamed as the inability to please his wife sexually. In a culture where men are often demasculinized, Camille Paglia has called the ability to achieve and maintain an erection "the last gasp of modern manhood." If a man suspects he can't become erect—or stay erect—he may avoid sex altogether rather than risk the humiliation. I've talked to some men in this situation who avoid sex because they don't want their wives to think they're not sexually exciting to them—even though that's exactly the message a guy sends when he avoids sex altogether.

If your husband seems disinterested in sex, he may be frustrated or in mourning over the perceived loss of a very important part of his life.

There's never a good time to be impotent, but if you had to choose a century to be impotent in, this is the one. New drugs and an increasing awareness of possible psychological causes have made most cases of impotence eminently treatable. It may be very difficult for your husband to express his fears on this subject, but I urge you to gently direct him toward seeing a doctor.

2. Excessive masturbation or use of pornography

I've talked with couples who have sex once or twice a month, even though the husband is having orgasms virtually every other day. If a man is pleasing himself constantly or using pornography, he may eventually lose interest in his wife. This is one of the great dangers of pornographic material. Eventually it can get in the way of a *real* sex life.

3. Sexual identity issues

Some men get married and start a family even though they sexually desire other men. If a man gets married hoping that the mere act of marriage will "change" him, he may be in for a surprise when, six or seven years later, he finds he has lost all interest in his wife. Worse, he may find the thought of sleeping with his wife to be repugnant.

A wife may not initially suspect homosexuality—after all, this man has fathered two or three children. But ignoring sexual orientation doesn't necessarily make it go away. If a man doesn't talk through his issues with a trained Christian counselor, it's likely that the pressure he feels inside will one day force itself to the surface.

Many men who have struggled with sexual identity enjoy satisfying sex lives with their wives, but they've had to work at it. And usually they've needed help from a Christian professional to help set things straight.

A word of warning: make sure you know the counselor. Some will tell the man to "stop living a lie" and pursue sexual relationships with other men. You want to find a counselor who is committed to a biblical view of sex and marriage.

4. Routine

If sex has become nothing more than a routine, it's only natural that sexual interest may flag somewhat. Surprise your husband with a new outfit or a suggestion to have sex in a new place. Do something to break out of the routine.

5. A willing but not eager wife

We've already covered this issue in some detail. You might be available for sex, but are you being enthusiastic about it? Remember the crucial difference between sex and sexual fulfillment.

6. Outside concerns

It's natural for a guy who just got a new computer to spend more time with his monitor than his wife. Other guys stay up late fixing antique cars. Still others get jazzed up about a new job. There are always going to be seasons when perfectly normal, healthy men get so excited about something else that sex seems less important. If you and your husband have enjoyed a fulfilling sexual relationship in the past, relax—he'll come back to you in time. Don't nag or push him farther away with accusations. Woo him back creatively. Drape lingerie over the steering wheel of the car he's working on. Drop a Polaroid picture into his briefcase before he leaves for work. Remind him of what he's missing and he'll come around.

We've pretty much covered the basics, so we're going to turn our attention to a few specifics. The following are some of the most common questions I receive in my practice.

Q: "Dr. Leman, what do you think about sharing sexual fantasies with my spouse?"

A: Sharing fantasies or sexual dreams can be a fun, healthy way to keep marital sex fresh and creative. God gave us our minds and imaginations, and there's no reason we can't use both to express our sexuality.

Q: "But is there a limit? How far is too far, fantasywise?"

A: As a Christian, I can easily answer that question. All fantasies should be about the marital couple. Any action that is moral to act out is moral to talk about. Any immoral action should not be talked about. Having three people in bed is not moral and thus is not an appropriate fantasy. Having sex with someone you're not married to is not moral, and Christian couples shouldn't go there.

Jesus said, "Whoever looks at a woman to lust for her has already committed adultery with her in his heart" (Matt. 5:28). There's no debate about this if you're a Christian; mental imagery can be tantamount to adultery.

Sex is a wonderful, beautiful thing. I think a husband and a wife should certainly push the envelope as they explore how to pleasure each other, but the exploration stops with them. Biblical sex is a two-person affair. There is no room in the marital bed for a third person, either real or imagined.

Q: "What if my husband wants me to do something sexually that I'm not sure about?"

A: You need to know your comfort level. A loving husband won't push you beyond that. But I want you to consider that comfort with new sexual expression is something you can grow into if you're willing.

Before I got married, the only vegetables I ate were peas and carrots—both of them out of the can. I certainly didn't spend much time in the produce aisle of my grocery store; instead, I made a beeline for the chips and ice cream. Now I regularly consume brussels sprouts, asparagus, spinach, and all kinds of green leafy mysteries.

Because I wanted to accommodate my wife, I learned to change my eating habits. You can do the same thing for your husband sexually. You may want to take it slow, but for the sake of your marriage, don't limit your comfort level to what it was when you were a virgin walking down the aisle.

The Bible is very explicit, particularly the Song of Songs. There is a great amount of freedom regarding what a husband and a wife can do in bed (provided you keep all sexual contact between the two of you). If something sounds distasteful to you, fine, but please don't make a moral case out of a personal preference. That's not fair to your husband. You shouldn't ever feel coerced to participate in something that you find repugnant, but learn to communicate this in such a way that you don't demean your husband's curiosity. Be ready with a backup: "You know what, Honey? I'm not sure I feel comfortable with that, but there's something else I can't *wait* to try."

Q: "But what about things like X-rated videos?"

A: Now we're approaching entirely different territory. I think it would be extremely difficult, if not impossible, for a Christian man to look at beautiful, naked models and not violate Matthew 5:28. It's best not to go there. Besides, virtually all of these movies present demeaning pictures of women. If a couple invited you over to watch them have sex, you'd refuse, and I don't see how it's any different to watch a couple through the lens of a camera.

If a wife is very inhibited, it might be helpful to watch some instructional videos, but I would categorically reject the use of blatant pornography.

Q: "What should a woman do if her husband wants her to do something that is immoral?"

A: I'm afraid such a situation is too common, even among Christians.

Your husband needs to know that you are committed to exploring your sexuality in all its fullness. Let him know—with actions as much as with words—that you are enthusiastic about your sex life and in growing together in that area.

Sexual hunger is progressive. When you start to go from intimate to kinky (see the next question), it's difficult to stop. Men who want their wives to watch pornographic movies with them will eventually start fantasizing about a threesome. And then they're likely to start talking about actually doing a threesome.

You must be firm here while working to sexually fulfill your husband. Don't just say no to the kinky; say an enthusiastic yes to appropriate sexual activity.

Some men (and women) feel that they need something illicit or immoral to enjoy sex. As a wife, you can't accommodate that. Your husband needs to get help if he equates "immoral" with "exciting."

Q: "What do you think constitutes *kinky?*"

A: Good question. I'm going to be very specific. Please understand, I'm not God's personal representative on this issue, but if you want me to don a striped suit and play the role of a referee (based on thousands of interviews with married couples), I'm willing to give it a shot.

Whenever you as a wife feel violated, you're probably coming close to kinky. Sex should draw you and your husband together, not push you apart. In my practice, a wife consulted me about her husband's request. He wanted her to provocatively undress in front of him while he masturbated. She was understandably disgusted by this selfish display of lust, and she was right to feel used in the process. There was no giving in this sexual situation—the man was pleasuring himself while treating his wife like a prop.

Another wife asked me if she was being "prudish" by refusing her husband's desire for anal sex.

"Absolutely not!" I told her. "Your body wasn't made for that!" Such a request certainly falls under the heading of kinky.

I've held the line in counseling sessions when men wanted their wives to don handcuffs. No wife should feel forced to endure demeaning behavior. It's no secret that some men like to dominate their wives, and this forced control can take many forms—such as a husband insisting that his wife swallow after oral sex. If you don't want to do this, then don't!

A wife needn't cater to a husband's perverted desires. One husband insisted on wearing his wife's pantyhose while they made love. She thought he looked silly and the whole exchange was sordid—and I wholeheartedly agreed with her.

While I think it is essential for married couples to expand their horizons, sexual expression must at all times be motivated by love, not lust. Paul was very clear that love "doesn't demand its own way." You are your husband's sexual partner, but you are not his sexual *slave*.

As we wrap up this part on marital sexuality, I need to stress once again that a wife should not feel compelled to do everything that her husband wants her to do. I don't believe that, I don't express that in the counseling room, and I certainly don't mean to imply that in this book. Our sex lives should be marked by love, maintained by love, and ruled by love—and love always takes into account the good, pleasure, and comfort of *both* partners. On the other hand, if you'll put a little more effort into practicing *healthy* sexuality, you may find that some of these other desires soon stop.

Well, that may be more than you wanted about how to please your husband sexually, but if you take it to heart, you'll have a very happy husband. A little effort on your part will go a long way, perhaps farther than you can imagine.

Just try it and see!

Communicating with Your Man

I'm going to be honest with you. Communication in marriage can be a minefield. Consider the titles of some of the bestselling books that have been published on it: *Men Are from Mars, Women Are from Venus; You Just Don't Understand;* and *That's Not What I Meant!*

There is a great deal of confusion and misunderstanding in this area, and it's not all the man's fault. For example, I've always wondered why a woman would ask a man who owns two pairs of shoes what pair of hers looks best with a burgundy outfit! A husband thinks, *When I go running, I wear the sneakers. When I go to work, I wear the black ones*. It's a rather simple equation. What do we know about comparing shades of burgundy?

Still, you women ask, even though we give you ample reason not to. Sande and I were going on a trip, and she walked out of the bedroom wearing brilliantly white shoes with huge (and I mean *huge*) diamond-shaped rhinestones, perhaps the most monstrous pair of foot coverings I had ever seen. If Liberace had been a woman, he would have worn these shoes.

"You're not wearing those shoes on the plane, are you?" I asked.

"Well, sure I am."

"You mean, you're going to wear those outside where people can *see* them? They look like something a showgirl in Las Vegas would wear."

Sande looked at me, pity in her eyes, and said, "Trust me, Lemey, these are hip."

As God is my judge, at least twenty women stopped us in the airport to say, "Oh, I *love* those shoes! Where'd you get them? They're *adorable!*"

I started rolling my eyes, once again accepting the fact that when it comes to fashion, my opinion doesn't mean diddly.

Like most men, I could wear the same outfit five days in a row (that is, if Sande would let me). Lest you think this makes me a philistine, allow me to inform you that Albert Einstein owned six identical gray suits.

I'm an Einstein with socks. If I find a design I like, I'll buy six pairs! I was in Germany once when I saw a pair of socks that really got me excited. I spent $144 buying multiple sets of the same pair of socks!

> **Leman's Law #26:**
>
> Don't expect your husband to give you an informed opinion on something he doesn't know much about. Some things are better discussed with your girlfriends, not your husband.

"I Don't Know"

A common complaint I hear from a woman is that when she asks her husband, "Is something bothering you?" he often replies, "I don't know," or "Nothing."

Of course, something is bothering him! And of course, he knows what it is! That's what makes this answer so frustrating to a wife. When a man answers "What's bothering you?" by saying, "Nothing," he really means, "I'm not going to tell you right now." When he says, "I don't know," he means, "I do know, but I don't want to tell you."

I can hear the scream coming onto the page: "*Why not?*" Here's why: a man doesn't work through problems verbally. When a woman is facing a difficult issue or trying to sort through her emotions, her inclination is to talk it out, but a man is more likely to want to *think it through* before he talks (and if he thinks it through well enough, he'll *never* want to talk about it because in his mind, it's solved). Some men think that if they ignore the problem or conflict, it will go away.

It's okay to press a little bit here. Without nagging, try touching him to open him up. If he does start talking, make sure you listen without passing judgment. If you get contentious with him, he'll shut up for good.

But if he's not ready to talk yet, give him time. Always remind yourself that a man may not foresee any relief in talking about a problem. To him, talking about a problem only enlarges it and makes it worse. Granted, a man may be a coward and want to hide from the problem. In either case, a man often views talking as a burden, not a cure. It's a threat more than it is a promise.

Leman's Law #27:
A man often views talking as a burden, not a cure.

Don't Forget You're Talking to a Man

Another major problem in husband-wife communication is that a woman may want to have conversations with her husband that resemble conversations with her girlfriends. This isn't going to happen. Your husband is a man, and men talk differently.

For instance, men by and large don't like their choices to be challenged. Women "should" on men a lot, and men don't like to be "should" on. You can improve the quality of your marriage by 20 percent if you avoid saying, "You should . . . ," to your husband.

These "shoulds" can crop up in the most benign places, even restaurants. I've heard two or three women spend fifteen minutes discussing a menu. They go through taste expectations, but also consider the all-important factors of price, fat content, and their vegetable intake for that day—all of which may launch them into an entirely new conversation on some herb, supplement, or the regularity of their bowel movements.

I don't hear men doing this. We make a choice and stick with it. And we don't appreciate having that choice challenged with "should." We like what we like. When Sande and I go to the Hungry Hunter, I order the Hawaiian chicken. It's a good meal—chicken, a little pineapple, and a little glaze with wild rice on the side. If I go to Caruso's, I get lasagna. I've gone there since 1962 and have never, *ever* ordered anything besides lasagna. I know it'll taste good, so why take any chances?

That's not good enough for Sande, who once asked me, "Why don't you try something new?"

She asked me that only once. I replied, "Well, how would you feel if I tried another wife?" As her eyes grew wide, I added, "Don't you see there can be some merit in my always preferring the same thing?"

When we go to another restaurant, Austin's, I always get a grilled ham and cheese sandwich with tomato soup. Sande "shoulded" me once there, too, and said, "You should get this," pointing to a different item on the menu.

"I don't like that," I said.

"Well, if you ordered this, then I could have a bite."

"Listen, Honey, if you want a bite of it, why don't you order it?"

You see, women like to share food. Men have a far more proprietary attitude. If two men are eating lunch together, it's not likely you'll see one reach over and grab something off the other's plate. And we *never* order in committee: "You get this, and I'll get that, and we'll split it."

How Not to Talk to Your Man

Women often tell me they want to talk with their husbands, but I've found that many of them really want to talk at their husbands. Quite frankly, to talk to a man, you need to learn to shut up, be nonjudgmental, and quit trying to interpret what he means. If you think all this sounds unfair or sexist, I'm not arguing with you. I'm telling you the facts. If you keep judging your husband and talk at him instead of with him, it's only a matter of time until hubby shuts up for good.

Then you may compound this by "shoulding" him and judging him even more—for not talking! "You should talk to me more! How come we never sit and chat with each other?"

Ah, the pit grows ever deeper.

> **Leman's Law #28:**
> A man is never going to talk if he thinks his wife will put him down.

One last point about talking to your man that is different from talking to your girlfriend. By and large, a man wants the bottom line. Cut the amount of prelude by approximately 90 percent, and you'll get it just about right. Instead of saying, "Honey, my mom went in and the doctor diagnosed varicose veins. She's going to have to get them stripped, which will make it very difficult for her to walk for a couple of weeks. As you know, she lives all alone now, and the only person who can help her is Mrs. Jenkins, who just visits twice a week, on Thursdays and Fridays. Mom's going to need more help than that."

Trust me, you've probably lost him by that point. Instead, try this: "Honey, my mom is having surgery next week and needs some time to recover. Do you mind if she stays with us for a few days?"

If he wants more information, he'll ask for it.

The Friendship Factor

I can't stress too much how important it is for men and women to have and to be friends for their emotional and spiritual health. When

I say this in seminars, people always ask me, "Well, what do you do to make friends? Should you have a lot of friends?"

My conclusion is, you don't work toward having a lot of friends. If you've got *one* friend in life to whom you can bare your soul and tell anything, then you're a lucky person. Most people don't have that. If you've got two or three close friends, you are *really* lucky.

You may be surprised to realize that if your husband had to make the choice, he'd probably pick *you* to be his closest friend. But a wife may undercut this friendship by talking to others.

> **Leman's Law #29:**
> What you communicate outside your marriage will greatly impact the communication within your marriage.

How often does your husband hear something about himself from one of your friends? If the answer is "never," you're doing a good job. If the answer is "once a month," you're looking for trouble. If the answer is "once a week," you might be looking at a divorce.

These conversations may seem harmless to you. Maybe you just "let slip" that you do 99.9 percent of the cooking in your house, so next time you're out with another couple, your husband hears, "Well, Jim, I know you don't like to cook, but maybe you can help Fred on the barbecue anyway?"

Jim is thinking, *How does she know I don't like to cook?* And he'll figure out the answer.

As soon as a man suspects that his wife isn't trustworthy with what he shares or who he is, the intimacy of that marriage is as good as over. One of the cruelest things you can do to your man is to spread his secrets around. As I was writing this book, I came across a news item about an internationally known singer getting a divorce from her internationally known athlete husband, and she told the press of her husband's penchant for wearing her thong underwear. Let me tell you—that marriage is over. Whether the singer intended it or not, she has totally estranged herself from her husband.

The Language a Man Understands

Okay, we've spent a lot of time talking about how you can better meet your husband's needs. How can you communicate in a way to make him more aware of your needs? How do you get your husband to do what you want him to do or to enjoy doing something you enjoy doing?

A classic situation is this: a man is watching television, a bowl of ice cream in his lap. You want to talk to him, but you've learned that speaking up while he's watching a show doesn't work very well, so you wait until there's a commercial.

There's just one problem. Hubby has the remote control right next to his knee. As soon as a commercial comes on, he's flipping the channels.

"Charlie," you say.

"Just a second, Honey," he responds. "I'm seeing if there's anything else on."

The catch-22 is that as soon as he finds something else that's on, he won't be available to talk because he'll actually be watching it.

What can you do?

Not all men are alike. Apart from talking with you and your husband, I can't provide you with a surefire method of communication, but I can speak generally, and in general, men like to be touched.

Let's say you want Charlie to come home from work a little earlier. He has been missing too many of the kids' games, and little Melanie has started to mention it.

First, you have to make sure he's listening. Just because your mouth is moving doesn't mean he's aware of it, regardless of how close to him you are. Even his saying, "Uh-huh," or occasionally grunting, as if he were following you, doesn't necessarily mean he's listening.

Slow down, discover his road map, and wait until you arrive at that destination. Let's say he's moved by touch. If that's the case, you want to start touching him—rubbing his back or neck, maybe giving him a head rub, or stroking his thigh—before you speak. Don't expect this to be instantaneous. Let him warm up a little. Eventually he'll come around.

Then you say in a very gentle voice, "Look, Charlie, I know you've been busy; I know your boss is very demanding and brutal." This disclaimer is important. You must convey that you understand the pressures he is under before you add anything else. Otherwise, you'll come across as another person adding more weight onto his already overburdened shoulders.

"But little Melanie has played in five soccer games already this season, and you haven't been to one of them. She's started asking me why her dad is never at her games—and the last time, there were tears in her eyes when she talked about it. It would mean so much to me and to her if you could make time in your schedule this Friday at five o'clock. I'd love you to pieces if you'd do it."

By using physical touch, you've opened his ears and softened the blow. That's why I often say that the segue into a man's mind is often physical.

One young wife explained how she coped with her husband on a shopping trip. Her husband hates shopping, but he had dutifully gone along with her for most of the afternoon until she could see he had all he could take. She had to go to one more store, however. She knew her husband would groan if she even suggested going into Target, so she got creative.

"Honey," she said in a conspiratorial tone, "come closer. I want to tell you something."

"What?"

"No, you have to come close. Nobody else can hear this."

Hubby leaned in really close. She then touched him, put her mouth right next to his ears so that it almost felt like a kiss, then seductively whispered, "If you go to just one more store with me, I'll _____ as soon as we get home."

She mentioned one of his favorite things to do in bed, which thereafter became known to them as the Target Special. They've never told anyone what the Target Special is, but whenever this wife wants her husband to do her a special favor, she knows exactly what to say. Sex and even titillation can open a man's ears like nothing else.

Sande used a different method with me. She loves to go to antique shops, which initially held zero interest for me. I thought most of the stores suckered the general public into wading through someone else's garbage (and highly overpriced garbage at that!). I'd drive Sande to the shops, but usually sit outside in the car listening to sports radio, reading the newspaper, or exercising my spiritual gift of beeping the horn when Sande was in a store.

Then one day I finished the paper and there was nothing on the radio, so I walked into the store and stumbled across some Lone Ranger stuff, including a secret decoder ring! (You remember—the plastic toy you'd buy by sending fifty cents and two cereal box tops to Battle Creek, Michigan.) I also found one of the Lone Ranger's silver bullets! (I still get chills when I hear the *William Tell Overture* and imagine that masked horseman saving all of humanity.) I was hooked, and the two of us regularly go to antique stores and yard sales together.

Let me tell you what Sande did right: she didn't "should" on me, she didn't drag me against my will, and she didn't verbally beat up on me for sitting in the car. She did the opposite. She thanked me for driving her. Instead of feeling condemned for sitting in the car and listening to the radio, I felt appreciated for getting out of the house. That made me want to please her again.

Try communicating your desires this way. Touch him and then say, "Honey, you know what would be really special to me? I know you don't like craft fairs, but would you consider coming with me this Saturday? I promise I won't make you go through every booth. You can sit and read the paper or just watch the people go by, and then we could go to a restaurant afterward. It would mean a lot to me if you'd do that."

The next weekend, you need to meet your husband halfway. It's a great thing for your husband and you to do things together, but are you willing to do things *he* likes? I go to antique shops with Sande, but she accompanies me to football games. When I'm sitting with Moonhead or Joe, I may not speak to Sande for the entire game (besides an occasional, "Honey, can I get you a coffee?"), but she's with me, and she's not complaining. Instead she sits and talks with a friend. Even though we're not talking a whole lot, I like having her there, and that's all the reason she needs to attend.

Summing Up

Let's go over all this once again. It's a natural desire for you to want to communicate more effectively with your husband, but don't try to turn him into your girlfriend. Save some things, such as fashion, to discuss with your friends.

Also remember that while you may feel a *need* to talk things through, your husband may view talking as more of an additional burden than a possible cure. Common blocks to marital conversation include "shoulding" on your husband and betraying his confidence. Since a man is a physical being, try opening his ears with your hands. Touch him to get him to begin listening, and keep touching to keep him listening.

If you apply these practices consistently and give your husband due time (remember Chapter 8!), eventually you'll find a much more satisfying level of verbal intimacy with your spouse.

A Man and His Ego

Yes, it's big. And, yes, it's quite fragile. It's also a key to what makes a man tick. I'm talking about the male ego.

A little girl sat on her father's lap, looked up at him with adoration dripping out of her eyes, and said in the sweetest voice, "Daddy, has anyone ever told you that you're the smartest, most wonderful man in the world?"

The dad felt his chest expand a good four inches, but modestly replied, "No, Honey, no one has."

"Then where did you get that idea?" she asked.

A child's perception can shoot daggers. (That's why I often say in my seminars, "We have met the enemy, and they are small.") The truth is, we men can indeed be childlike when it comes to our egos. As vain as this might sound, you need to know the straight truth.

This law helps to explain why so many men have such a difficult time when they feel as if they've lost their wives to their babies. This battle never ends. The husband sees his wife knock herself out for the kids, and by the end of the day she's too exhausted for him. And the husband may take this personally.

Leman's Law #30:
Men want to be the centerpiece of their wives' attention.

As a wife, you naturally don't understand this: "They're *your* kids, too, after all. I'm doing this for you." This makes perfect sense, but the problem is, you're thinking like a woman, not like a man. It doesn't touch on the *emotional slight* that the husband feels.

Remember, it's not about fairness. It's not about a proper division of labor. It's not even about child rearing. It's about his ego.

That also helps to explain why that husband of yours is so reluctant to stop and ask for directions even when he's hopelessly lost. He doesn't think it's beneath him to ask for directions; he's not too proud to acknowledge that he's lost; he doesn't love the challenge of figuring it out. The answer is much simpler than that—he doesn't want to let all those cars that he spent hours passing to catch up and pass *him* by!

Though we may look like men, inside every man is a little boy who loves his toys, his sports—and being the center of your attention. If you don't become more familiar with the male ego, you'll never fully understand your husband.

Bravado

In February 1964, a twenty-two-year-old kid named Cassius Clay faced one of the most terrifying nights of his life. He was scheduled to box World Heavyweight Champion Sonny Liston, a giant of a man who had knocked out Floyd Patterson *twice*. I'm sure most of the women reading this book don't have any idea who Patterson was, but before Patterson fought Liston, nobody thought he could be beaten, much less knocked out, and certainly nobody could imagine a fighter strong enough to knock him out *twice* in two different bouts.

That's why Sonny Liston was such a huge favorite to absolutely demolish Cassius Clay (who would later be known as Muhammad Ali). The betting establishment gave Liston 9–1 odds, and commentators said, with half seriousness, that Clay's ringside physician "better have some postmortem experience."[1] At best, the fight was considered a gross "mismatch." At worst, some people thought the young Clay would be seriously hurt.

There's little doubt that Clay was terrified. The doctor who examined him before the bout was shocked at Clay's soaring blood pressure. He quietly told a few colleagues, "This fighter is scared to death."

Yet Clay responded to the pressure and his own fears with typical male braggadocio. He drove up to Liston's house shortly before the fight and shouted out to him from the sidewalk. That was terribly insulting to Liston. The heavyweight champion had only recently moved into the quiet, white-collar neighborhood where such things just "didn't happen."

At the weigh-in, Clay acted like a nut. He looked as if he hated Liston and couldn't wait to get his hands on him. He had to be physically restrained from charging after Liston right then.

During the fight introductions, with the first round seconds away, Clay sneered into his bigger opponent's face and said, "I've got you now, Sucker." A bruising battle ensued, but at the end of the night, Clay won one of the most famous bouts in boxing history.

There's a story behind this fight, however. Later in life, Ali (Clay) admitted that all of the prefight shenanigans—the whole bit about screaming at Liston from the sidewalk and acting like a lunatic during the weigh-in—was part of a carefully calculated plan. Said Ali, "Liston's not afraid of me, but he's afraid of a nut."

The brilliant idea was this: Ali knew his smaller body would never strike fear into the heart of his bigger opponent. He also knew he was less experienced than Liston. He had no hope of intimidating Liston through typical tactics, so he switched gears and tried unusual tactics. Ali wanted Liston to think he was about to fight a man who was absolutely crazy. If Ali could make Liston think that his opponent was really off his rocker, who knows what might happen? And that little question might be enough to give the younger fighter the opening he needed to pull off one of the greatest upsets in all of boxing history. Ali demonstrated what is true of most men. He'd rather be known as a braggart or a crazy man than a coward.

When your husband seems aloof and distant; when you see your son acting crazy around other kids in the neighborhood; when your father refuses to look reality in the face and becomes forceful if you mention his selling his house and moving into a nursing home, perhaps there's a simple explanation: maybe he's scared to death, and he doesn't want to admit it.

I don't care how long you've known your husband or how humble he is, it will *never* be easy for him to admit he's afraid. If your husband is watching his business slowly slide into bankruptcy; if your son is terrified about whether girls will think he's attractive; if your father is scared silly watching himself age into an inevitable period of needing to be cared for, all three might well respond by becoming more arrogant, more flashy, and more stubborn. Instead of retreating and asking for help, they'll likely think they should charge ahead and see what happens.

Here's the catch: your husband's mother might never have taught him how to positively face a crisis in his confidence. Every man will eventually face such a challenge, but if he hasn't been properly prepared to do so, he can be an absolute bear to live with. You'll notice that something is wrong with your husband, but you'll never be able to get him to open up about it, largely because we men tend to run from self-disclosure if we think that self-disclosure will make us look weak.

Though males like to look tough on the outside, we can be cream cheese on the inside, particularly when we face one of the most difficult seasons of life—the midlife crisis.

The Midlife Morass

I've got some sobering news for you. The midlife crisis isn't a myth. Men really do go through a time of questioning and reevaluating in their forties and fifties. They can be very vulnerable years. I've seen godly men do the most ungodly things, including leaving their wives, grabbing new honeys, and wrecking their reputations.

Even godly men act in ways that probably would offend you. When things get tense, we joke about it. For example, my good buddy Moonhead and I often go out on a boat called *The Fat Chick Magnet.*

The boat got its name because Moonhead and I realized that if we could pick up chicks (which we wouldn't), they'd have to be old and fat. If you're offended, I'm not surprised. Women can't understand how men on the far side of middle age come to grips with thinning hair, gaining weight, and losing all semblance of sex appeal. We joke about it! We can get crude. We do everything except what women do—get personal. We don't talk about it—we laugh about it! We're Cassius Clay, pretending we're not scared of what's happening, when all the while we might be terrified about the changes taking place. Please try to be empathetic here; this is just how males respond. You may not like it, but I want you to understand it.

One time Moonhead and I were talking: "You know we're getting old when we stop looking at the chicks and start looking at their mothers—and the mothers look good to us!"

Unfortunately the nature of the male ego is tailor-made to erupt during the midlife morass. When a man gains his identity and sense of self-worth primarily outside the home and his dreams don't come true, he is suddenly very vulnerable. He knows that every new man he meets is virtually guaranteed to ask him within about thirty seconds, "What do you do for a living?" If the answer is something he's not proud of, this question can feel like a body slam.

To top it off, if the guy's marriage is suffering, or if he feels that his sex life is going nowhere or is nonexistent, disaster isn't far away. His ego will accept a bruise here and there, but eventually it's going to fight back.

I know of a famous family crusader who spoke out forcefully and powerfully in defense of the unborn and of human values. He argued on national television and radio shows against the breakdown of family values and worked tirelessly to defeat special privileges granted to homosexuals.

After a turn of events left him extremely disappointed and nearly penniless, and after he poured his energy into a cause only to have that cause rebuffed, the man fell apart, left his wife and children, and became part of the problem instead of part of the solution.

Here's what's going on: most men harbor dreams from their teens and early twenties about what life will be like in their forties. Few of those dreams will come true. The realization hits a man at precisely the time when he realizes his energy has decreased, his life has become routine, and he is in far worse shape physically than he has ever been in his life.

These men walk into my office all the time. Now here's the *really* dangerous truth: the same phenomenon hits women as frequently as it does men, leading to disastrous situations.

A recent case involved a superwoman in her late forties. She is the type of woman who organizes annual events at school, helps keep the church going, is successful in business, and still manages to decorate her house for every holiday season.

Her husband, on the other hand, felt as if he was "spinning his wheels." His job was going nowhere, and he was very noncommunicative with his wife—a typical uptight, ego-driven husband facing a severe midlife morass.

I listened with empathy as this woman told me through tears how unhappy she was. Once there was a break, I knew I had to offer a warning.

"Do you realize you're headed toward an affair?"

"Wrong," she said almost too quickly. "I've already had one. It lasted two years and I feel terrible about it."

Superwoman wanted a superhusband, not a loser facing a crisis in his confidence. She knew her affair wasn't going anywhere, but admitted, "I deceived myself with the thought that I deserved to be loved by somebody."

The challenge is that just when you need an extrasupportive husband, your sweetheart may be less talkative, less affectionate, and less communicative than he ever has been. He's fighting his own demons, leaving you to feel that you're utterly alone.

> **Leman's Law #31:**
> During a midlife transition, just when you need an extrasupportive husband, your sweetheart may be less talkative, less affectionate, and less communicative than he ever has been.

If I were writing this book for men, I'd have a long chapter about how husbands can support their wives during this difficult transitional time. But since this book is written for women, I'm going to provide you with a few tips for the care and feeding of the male ego.

Helping Your Man Age

At thirty-seven years old, Jerry Rice has a lot of life left ahead of him, but not much football. He is without question the greatest wide receiver in NFL history, holding virtually every record a wide receiver can hold. But in the 1999 season, he noticed that teams started playing him differently. They didn't fear him quite the way they used to, and that hurt. In previous years, they'd put their best cornerback on him or even double-team him; in 1999, he often received far less attention than did the other receivers on his team.

"Over the years," he told a reporter for *Sports Illustrated*, "I have always—*always*—been a factor. Now it's like I'm not there. Now maybe I get one ball in the first half, two or three in the second half. To not be a factor, that's the toughest thing."[2]

As men age, egos become all the more sensitive because we literally see parts of ourselves slipping at the same time that we see long-cherished dreams crushed. One man remarked how a watershed event in his life occurred when he realized he was "invisible" to college-age women. Most of us men still think of ourselves as being a few years out of college. We might be a tad slower, but we're hanging on to the illusion that we can shoot a jump shot with the best of them.

Two or three decades later, after our hair has begun thinning and we realize a potbelly is going to be a permanent fixture, we know we will never again turn a woman's head by our swagger or our looks—at least not in a positive way.

It's not an easy admission.

You can give your husband a great gift during this transition by being very deliberate in your communication. When your husband starts to lose his hair, for instance, every time he looks in the mirror he might be thinking, *Will my wife learn to love a bald man?*

Your compliments on his physical appearance mean more than you know. If someone good-naturedly comments on your husband's thinning hair, say something like, "Hey, I *like* this head." If your husband mentions his bulging stomach, pat it gently and say, "But I *like* it; it's mine!"

Let him know that as each year goes by, you're falling more and more in love with him. Make sure he hears how much he turns you on. You may very well appreciate the way he treats your children far more than you appreciate his sex appeal, but *he* still wants to hear that he's sexually appealing.

If your husband is like most men, his vocational reality will not be close to his vocational dreams. During this time, tell him regularly what a great provider he is and how much you appreciate his hard work on your and the kids' behalf. Most of us men don't mind working hard, but we want to feel we're appreciated for doing it.

Another thing you can do is to focus on what your husband did right—even if it cost him. Remind him that yes, turning down that one job impeded his advancement in the company, but you really appreciate how he allowed the kids to grow up in the same neighborhood without having to move every three years. Yes, he might have earned a few more bucks if he had stayed late and worked weekends, but you truly appreciate how he reserved time for the family. Remember—his bosses won't thank him for putting his family first. If you don't thank him, *no one will*, and he might be tempted to question his sacrifice.

As you build up your husband, make sure you mention that you're proud of him not just for what he does, but for who he is. You need to do the former, but don't neglect the latter. Give him verbal strokes for being honest, hardworking, kind, benevolent, and gentle—someone you are proud to be married to and someone the kids are proud to have as a dad.

Never forget that inside the big man is a little boy who needs to feel needed. If the world doesn't applaud him—and it usually won't—he needs your approval and appreciation.

My wife, Sande, has been excellent at affirming both what I've done and who I am. She did both in one present after my first book was published. I opened up a framed copy of the cover featuring the words *Number one husband, Number one father, Number one author*. Of course, I was proud to have a book published; but what Sande did turned my affection back to my family, keeping me from being lured into putting more attention into publishing than being a husband and a dad.

Communicating with the Male Ego

Laura spoke for many wives when she asked me, "Why does a man think that unless something is *his* idea it can't be worthwhile or good?"

When you are communicating with the male ego, timing and listening are all-important. You'll have to learn to encourage rather than dictate, and then occasionally wait until the man's common sense catches up with yours.

How do you do that? You feed the man bits and pieces of information so that he naturally draws the conclusion you already had in mind. By the way, I teach this approach to men as well as to women. Male subordinates have to learn how to deal with male boss egos, too, you know!

If the man's ego is a huge problem, you probably aren't going to change it, so you need to learn how to work around it. Let's say, for instance, that you are exhausted trying to eke a few more loads out of a washing machine that has clearly cleaned its last clothes, but you know your husband won't react too well to your suggestion that you buy another washer.

If you really want a new washer, you may need to stroke your husband's ego and approach him like this: "John, I don't know what you want to do about this, but the Sears repairman came out today and said that the washer is just about shot. He said it'll cost us about $300 to fix it. I don't know finances the way you do, but do you think it makes more sense to buy a new one for $375?"

Obviously the wife knows it doesn't make sense to spend $300 fixing a washer when a new one costs $375, but when she plays this game, she's not demeaning herself. She's adjusting to what *is*. Her husband's weakness, not hers, necessitates this approach. Understanding this—and making allowances for it—is a sign of *strength*. You may hate this suggestion and be offended by it, but it's really a matter of being practical. Do you want to get the new washer?

When people come into my office for counseling, my goal is to help them learn how to better relate to each other. But I've been around enough couples to know that sometimes, a woman is married to a man who will *never* change. In those instances, I'm going to teach her how to survive and thrive—including how to get a new washer.

We must address one more aspect of the male ego: you may not realize it, but if you're like most women, you violated your marital vows within the last thirty days. And when you did so, you made a very dangerous assault on your husband's fragile ego.

How Women Happily Violate Their Vows

You know where most wives violate their marital vows? It's not inside a lover's bed. It's not at some out-of-the-way "no tell motel." It's not even in their minds. It's during weekly Bible studies.

Those places can be cauldrons of gossip. Once the warm-ups (children) are dispensed with, women move on to the main course—complaining about husbands. Such unfaithfulness isn't limited to Bible studies; the telephone and now Internet chat rooms have created enormous, round-the-clock opportunities for women to violate their marital vows all day long.

Let's get the facts out of the way. Wives will speak, on average, three and one-half times the amount of words that their husbands speak on any given day. They have to speak those words to *somebody*, and they have to use those words to describe *someone*. Since hubby isn't as comfortable using words, it's very likely that Martha will call up Mabel and have it out with her—and it won't take long until Mabel finds out that, yes, can you believe it, Herbert wanted it *again* last night.

In these situations, women invariably do a lot of comparing, just as they compare their children. Some may be saying, "I wish my husband helped out like that," while others will think or even say out loud, "I'm glad my husband doesn't do *that!*"

Let's apply the same logic to another situation. What would you say if your husband had an affair and used the justification, "You won't have sex with me as much as I want it, so why can't I have sex with somebody else?"

> **Leman's Law #32:**
> Men hate it when their wives talk about them behind their backs, but they rarely tell their wives they hate it.

You're expected to know this. To the male mind, the fact that a guy wouldn't like this seems so obviously apparent that he believes he shouldn't have to mention it.

Four Types of Terrible Talk

Men, by nature of our egos, are private creatures. We don't like people to know our secrets, but many wives can't seem to keep these secrets to themselves.

Joanne Kaufman wrote an interesting article for *Redbook* magazine entitled "Let's *Not* Talk About Sex."[3] She began her article with a classic description of marital violation: "A friend just called to tell me, in the absolute strictest confidence, of course, that her husband has a seriously low sperm count." She did *not* want to know this, and she felt that knowing it put her in an extremely difficult situation: "I now live in mortal dread that the next time I see this guy, I'm going to use the words, 'shooting blanks' and 'lies there like a lox' in the same sentence."

Kaufman confirmed what I have long suspected—that gossip among women is at an all-time high: "Over the past several years I've been the receptacle for so many of my friends' connubial—and in some cases, extra-connubial—confidences that I have enough data to rewrite Kinsey."

She noticed four types of gossip: (1) the outright boast, (2) the boast disguised as a complaint ("John just can't get enough of me; I don't know when I'm ever going to get any sleep"), (3) the complaint ("I wonder if they make extra-strength Viagra"), and (4) the confession.

Not one of these is appropriate—and not just for the sake of your husband. If you're bragging about how often you and the old man get it on, how do you think that makes a woman feel who can't remember the last time she and her husband slept together?

If you insist on talking to someone else about your marriage, try talking to God!

There may be one exception. If you have an exceptionally close friend with whom your husband feels comfortable, you might be able to talk to her, *provided you ask your husband's permission first*. My wife, Sande, knows she can talk to Wendy, my best friend Moonhead's wife. But don't be surprised if your husband says no. You shouldn't be surprised if he's offended that you asked! That's how private a man can be. He might feel betrayed by the mere thought that you considered talking to someone else about him, so tread carefully here.

Keep in mind, it is *never* appropriate to discuss your husband in a group setting. I'm all for Bible studies, but use the time to discuss Scripture, not your husband!

I hope this discussion of the male ego didn't scare you. There's no question that the male ego is a fragile and sensitive thing, but if you play it right, you can use it to your advantage. When your husband has his ego needs met at home; when you compliment him and build him up during the difficult midlife transition; when you respect his privacy and guard his insecurities, you create a very loyal and positive husband. The same force that can tear your marriage apart can keep pushing the two of you together. You just have to channel it in the right direction.

PART 4

Men You Don't Have to Live With (but Who Still Drive You Crazy)

Men at Work

Did you hear about Greg? He got the new position as district manager."

Anne breathed a sigh of surprised relief. Greg had always had a wary disregard for management. He often blew off meetings when he knew they had no purpose, and he openly despised bureaucratic regulation, so Anne was confident he wouldn't be heavy-handed now that he was in authority.

She couldn't have been more wrong. The same man who had openly disdained rules two weeks ago began passing more rules than anybody in his position ever had. When Anne tried to kid with him, Greg pulled her aside and said in a firm voice, "Anne, I won't have you disagreeing with me in front of my subordinates!"

"Your *subordinates?*" Anne asked. "Two weeks ago you called these people your *friends!*"

Learning to handle men at work is second in difficulty only to handling thirty unruly kindergartners. So many issues get piled on top of each other that it can be an absolute minefield trying to work with men. Since you can't change the men you work with (if you try, you'll only frustrate yourself), I'm going to offer some advice for how to dance around their little peccadilloes.

> **Leman's Law #33:**
> You can't change men at work, but you can manage them.

To begin with, I need to make one thing absolutely clear. If you want a promotion; if you want to succeed in your company; if you want the men under your supervision to perform their best, you'd better listen to what I have to say.

You must accept this limitation. Work relationships are limited. It is not your place to try to make someone relax more, learn to be kinder, or become more sensitive. You are hired to get a task done, and that task will usually require that you learn how to work with others. Put any thought of changing others out of your mind. You have to learn how to work *around* their weaknesses.

No doubt some of my faithful readers have been wondering, *So, when is Leman going to get around to birth order this time?* Here it is. Not all men are alike, but most men of certain birth orders are remarkably similar. Understanding their inclinations will give you a big head start toward working more effectively with them.

While it is possible that a lastborn will sometimes take on the characteristics of a firstborn (particularly if there is a large age gap or if the older sibling is an extreme in one direction or another, forcing the lastborn to "overtake" him), becoming familiar with a person's most likely inclination is one of the most valuable skills in the office. If you're one of those bosses (or subordinates) who thinks everybody can (and should) be treated in the same way, I guarantee you're a very frustrated woman. You can't treat everybody the same way because people don't act the same way. We have different motivations and different perspectives on life, based in large part on our family of origin.

That's all very fine, Dr. Leman, you may be thinking, *but* how *do I find out a man's birth order?* Unless you know someone really well, you probably can't start a conversation by asking, "Are you a firstborn?" Besides, you don't want to give away what you're doing. It might even sound manipulative to the uninitiated.

Instead, listen for clues in a typical conversation. For example, let's say a male coworker casually mentions, "My brother and I went fishing the other day."

You respond, "Oh, you have a brother?"

"Yeah."

"Is he older? Younger?"

"He's my baby brother."

"Do you have any other siblings?"

That's a natural progression in a conversation. Once you're armed with this information, you can apply the following strategies as you work with firstborn Frank, middle-born Mike, and lastborn Louie. (If you're a stay-at-home mom, by the way, you'll still find this information useful as you raise your sons and interact with other men in church and social settings.)

Firstborn Frank

Asking a firstborn—who already tends to be bossy and opinionated—*why?* immediately puts him on the defensive. He'll see it as an indirect challenge to his sense of control, and once a firstborn is suspicious, your chances of persuading him of some other way of doing things is almost nonexistent.

Leman's Law #34:

Never ask a firstborn at work why?

Firstborns are natural leaders. They represent U.S. presidents, astronauts, and CEOs by overwhelming numbers. They often live with a sense of entitlement and superiority.

You can make three fatal mistakes with a firstborn male at work. First, if you really want to fail with your boss or create tremendous resentment with a subordinate, act like a know-it-all. That'll really make a firstborn competitive and mark you out as a primary threat. Second, be pushy. That'll thoroughly get him riled, particularly since firstborns aren't used to being challenged. Third, don't be well organized or assemble any facts to back up your statements. Approach firstborn Frank largely with feelings and emotions, and you'll drive him crazy (and make him lose all respect for you).

With a firstborn male, you must never fake a presentation. This man tends to be a black-and-white thinker with a high level of discernment. If you're not organized or if you don't know what you're talking about, he'll find out soon enough—and write you off as "all sizzle and no steak." Worse, because he is a black-and-white thinker, you'll have an extremely difficult time ever getting him to change his opinion of you. Once he labels you, you'll have to stop the world from turning to get him to look at you any differently.

Another tip: don't surprise a firstborn male. He *hates* surprises. Keep him apprised of what you're doing, and make sure he feels part of the process if that's appropriate. If you can foresee a time when you may have to fire a firstborn male, create a paper record so that he can see it coming. If you're a subordinate who sees that you're going to have to deliver some bad news (maybe you'll miss a deadline, for instance), keep your firstborn male boss in the loop. Ask for his opinion or advice along the way; don't blindside him with a problem when it's too late to solve it.

Although you'll hate me for saying this, a firstborn male needs his ego stroked at work. I'm not saying this is a good thing; I'm just trying to help you deal with what is. However, when you stroke his ego, don't use empty flattery. As strange as this may seem, you must be able to back up any compliment. Remember, a firstborn has high discernment and won't tolerate insincere praise.

An effective method of closing a sale with a firstborn male is to use oppositional attraction. With this method, you are honest about negative points as well as positive points, and then you give him options he can choose from. You may be wondering, *Why would I want to point out the downside of this deal or that decision?* The answer is that your candor will earn great favor with the firstborn male. Once he understands that you're not trying to pull one over on him, he's going to be much more comfortable making a decision—and a firstborn male *loves* to make decisions. (Besides, if he's a normal firstborn, he'll see the flaw anyway and become suspicious that you're trying to hide it.)

Middle-Born Mike

What you need to know about middle-born Mike, first and foremost, is that he's very relational, he is probably a pleaser, and more than likely he isn't too fond of confrontation. He will tend to be less ambitious than Frank, but much more desirous than Frank of having everybody like him—or at least be happy with him.

I know one young middle-born man who had a very respectable position in management, but he hated it. He didn't like having people "under him." He *hated* having to confront them, goad them, or deliver bad news, so he finally admitted that management wasn't for him and became a mail carrier. People love to see him walking their way, and older women occasionally stop him for a brief chat. He's the "light" in the neighborhood and couldn't be happier with his new job.

That's not unusual for a middle born, who is usually a good team player, reliable, steady, and loyal. There are exceptions—sometimes a middle born will be a scrappy, ambitious climber, just aching to pull down firstborn Frank.

When you work with Mike, keep the relationship up front. Don't jump right into business. Ask him about his weekend, and spend a few minutes going over his social life. Mike wants to be your friend. Let him.

Mike will not be as comfortable making decisions as Frank is. He'll doubt himself more, so he'll need more time to change his previous way of thinking. Don't expect him to sign on to a completely new idea the first time you present it to him. You may have to follow the Rule of Seven.

The Rule of Seven suggests that to change someone's mind, you should anticipate seven different conversations. The purpose of the first conversation is to bring up the idea so that it will begin to sound familiar. You're not trying to do any convincing; you're broaching the subject: "Hey, Mike, I heard of this new office building that has cut-rate leases. It looks like a great new building." That's *it.* Don't take it any farther.

The second time, you add more information: "Mike, I've been thinking. Remember that new office building I told you about?"

"Yeah."

"Since it's a little farther out from the city, do you think it might cut down on some of our commutes to work?"

Your goal is to slowly add a little more information each time you bring up the new office building. By the seventh time, Mike will finally be comfortable enough with the idea to seriously consider it. Firstborn Frank will want to see the numbers, with a list of the pros and cons, during the first meeting. Mike needs to take more time to grow accustomed to possible change.

Whatever you do with Mike, don't be confrontational. That's a sure recipe for disaster. If you become too pushy, Mike will shut you off and avoid you. If you work for a Mike, you'll need to get used to the idea that some things won't be addressed. Mike may not immediately jump in and solve every problem. The positive is that you and your fellow subordinates will have far more freedom working for Mike than you would have working for Frank. The negative is that you can't count on as much structure or top-down support. You're going to have to solve many disputes.

Mike likes recognition. If you're Mike's boss, send him a congratulatory e-mail when he deserves it or give him a certificate to hang up in his cubicle. Recognize his accomplishments, and he'll go out of his way to please you again in the future. If Mike is your boss, sincerely congratulate him when he steers your department through a significant accomplishment. Let him know that you enjoy working for him and respect his leadership. A little bit of time spent on the relationship will go a long way toward winning over middle-born Mike.

Lastborn Louie

A lastborn has spent his entire life trying to draw more attention to himself. He is often the performer, the class clown, the life of the party. He will take far more risks than his conservative oldest sibling, but instead of conquering the world, he usually wants to enjoy it.

With a lastborn, few things work as well as emotional charm. For a first business contact, it's preferable to arrange a social setting. Have a couple of good jokes ready (but don't use off-color humor). You'll want to keep the presentation moving—the baby's attention span is short—so bring your "dancing" shoes and prepare to entertain Louie.

Name-dropping invariably works with a lastborn. Louie is most likely to be impressed that someone he looks up to and respects is using this product or agrees with your decision. "You know, Louie, Frank in accounting told me he thinks this is really the way to go. What do you think?" A little flash and glitter will help any presentation, but don't let your lightness give a hint of a lack of respect (which a lastborn is already sensitive about anyway).

A lastborn tends to be impetuous; you may have to press him to get a decision. And if you take too long to make your case, forget it. Louie has a very short attention span. He gets bored rather easily, so do yourself a favor and break up a long presentation into bits, scheduling two or three meetings instead of one.

Whereas Frank wants to see the steak and not the sizzle, Louie *likes* the sizzle. Showy charts, loud illustrations, and fancy packaging tend to work with a lastborn man. The sizzle keeps his attention and encourages him to more seriously consider what you're proposing.

If what you're suggesting involves major change, you're going to have much more success with Louie than with Frank. If you're trying to build a consensus, go to Louie first, slowly cultivate Mike, and then present the hard facts to Frank.

One final word about Louie: by virtue of his birth order, Louie is already suspicious that others don't respect him. Be very careful about saying or doing anything that confirms this suspicion. Be friendly with Louie, crack jokes, but make sure you don't cross a line that could in any way be misconstrued as a lack of respect. If you remind Louie that he's a lastborn, you've lost him.

Dealing with Male Bosses

No one ever said working for men is easy. Dancing around our egos, understanding our motivations, and not inadvertently insulting us can take the wisdom of Solomon and the patience of Job. There's a simple explanation. If you ask most men (particularly those who don't consider themselves religious) where they get the majority of their self-esteem, work is at the top of the list. Consequently, if you're a subordinate who makes your boss look bad, he'll never forgive you. On the other hand, if you help him to succeed, he'll take you all the way to the top.

Let's look at a few management styles you might meet. Add these insights to your boss's birth order, and you'll have a good understanding of how to survive and thrive in the workplace.

The White-Banded Barfly

The name of the white-banded barfly comes from the white band on the barfly's ring finger. He's liable to take off his wedding ring when he thinks the situation is favorable for a little extramarital dalliance.

This boss won't be shy about trying to pick you up. He may begin his flirtations with inappropriate comments, or he may jump right in and speak in a rank, gross, and filthy manner. He's a prime target for a sexual harassment lawsuit, but that rarely seems to stop him.

Today, I find the white-banded barfly is most often in a family business; he's the firstborn son and has always had power and a strong sense of entitlement. At fifty-two years old, he's gone through two wives and is well on his way to a third because he has no appreciation for women.

Even if you make it clear that you don't welcome the barfly's advances, he'll try to take liberties—though they may be nonsexual. Instead, they'll be something like this: "By the way, Schnooks, I need you to get this out tonight. Can you stay late?"

"But, Andy," you protest, "my husband and I have company coming over tonight."

"I'm sure they'll understand. Make sure this is on my desk before you leave. And call Rod. Tell him I'm going to be fifteen minutes late to the golf course."

You must build parameters for a white-banded barfly. When he asks you to come over to his place at odd hours or you suspect he has reserved one room when the two of you are traveling together, stand up straight and say, "No!" Ambiguity with this guy will work against you; make sure there isn't any chance that he could take any of your words in the wrong way.

Although standing up to the barfly can be dangerous, another principle will work in your favor when you refuse to bow down to his every whim, and that is Leman's Law #35:

Leman's Law #35:

Powerful people respect other people's power. They may not like other people's power, but they will respect it.

Your power comes not from position, but from self-respect. If you lose this sense of self-respect, you've lost everything. The white-banded barfly will run all over you.

With the barfly as your boss, you'll have to set limits on your exertion of power. For instance, your barfly makes a snide remark that is clearly inappropriate or suggestive. Simply say, "I didn't appreciate that," and then turn and walk out the door. That's exerting power in an appropriate way. If you push the barfly too far, however, your career with that company is doomed.

In this day and age, *you* as a woman have the legal power. Lawyers now tell me that the *only* legal place for a male boss to touch a female employee is between her wrist and elbow. You may be open to more than that, but know your parameters. As a further act of self-protection, make sure your job description is black and white so that the barfly can't concoct a contrived reason for firing you. Fulfill your assigned duties flawlessly, *carefully watch your dress*, and above all else, don't try to outtalk him with suggestive words of your own. If someone else hears you, you can bet the barfly's defense lawyers will put him on the stand, and your character will be annihilated in a public court of law. You'll come out sounding like the loosest woman who has ever held down a job.

You have to respect yourself. A barfly preys on women with low self-esteem. If you're working for a barfly, the ultimate statement of self-respect is to get another job, which I recommend. This man never changes. Your only real option is to leave when the situation he creates becomes unbearable.

The Controlling Dictator

The controlling dictator is extremely hard to work for. He demands perfection, hates to be told that he is wrong, and is usually adept at casting blame. Even when he clearly makes a mistake, he is skilled at making the mishap look as if it's someone else's fault. To add insult to injury, he is equally skilled at taking credit for a subordinate's good work.

If you work for a man like this, you're probably not going to like what I'm about to say, but keep in mind something I said at the start of this chapter: *you can't change men at work, but you can manage them.* To keep your job, you must learn to keep the peace. That means you must occasionally take the hits for this guy and, just as painful, watch him steal your glory. For your mental health, you must learn to do this while not taking it personally. A controlling dictator does this to everybody, not just you. You happen to be the most recent person he has the opportunity to use and abuse.

A controlling dictator is most often a firstborn, so remember that he doesn't like surprises. You must be extremely organized, even to the point of anticipating problems that *might* arise. Never let this boss see you at a loss for what to do. Even better, learn how to shield him from misfortune. Here's the cold, hard truth when you're working for a controlling dictator: he'll love your loyalty, but if you cross him, you're dead.

Because a controlling dictator is driven, he'll expect you to be equally driven. He won't think twice about asking you to forgo picking up your daughter from the skating rink and staying late to perfect his presentation.

In short, you must establish parameters, or he'll eventually establish them for you. In time, you won't *have* a personal life. This guy will take and take and then take some more. Yet even after years of your undying loyalty, cross him once, and you'll be written out of his life faster than you can blink.

This man has an extremely narcissistic personality; everything is always going to be about *him.* Either you learn to work with that reality, or you have to find a new job.

The People Pleaser

Compared to working for the barfly or the controlling dictator, it might sound refreshing to work for the people pleaser (most likely a middle born who has somehow been placed in management). After all, he's a nonconfronter, so he never yells at you. He'll go out of his way to please you, even though he's your boss. What's the downside?

This man will never stand up and fight for you. If you desperately need a new copier, he'll promise you for ten years that he's going to demand that you get one, but at the first sign of resistance, he'll turn tail and run. He says yes to everybody but rarely delivers.

The other downside is that if your future is tied to a people pleaser, you'd better not plan on climbing very high. A people pleaser will rarely get beyond middle management.

To work with this guy, you may need to make a few decisions for him. He'll rarely confront problems among his subordinates, so you're going to have to learn how to settle disputes.

While I'm not a complete people pleaser, by virtue of my birth order (lastborn), I'm far more like this than I am, say, the controlling dictator or the barfly. Fortunately I have an extremely competent (firstborn) assistant named Debbie who knows how to handle me. She lines up everything for me and says, "Okay, Kevin, you need to do this and this and this," and I do it.

Sometimes I'll ask, "Debbie, do I really need to do this?"

"Yes, Kevin, you do."

I may sigh my displeasure, but I'll probably do it. From the day I hired Debbie, I told her that I pay her to think. I ask for her input and value it. That's the advantage of working for a people pleaser—you know you're needed.

Remember that a people-pleaser boss is usually going to be worried about failing; *your job is to try to get him to start thinking about succeeding.* Otherwise he'll always take the safe route, never risk, and rarely get anything done beyond preserving the status quo.

The Hovercraft

This boss makes you wish you had a can of Business Raid—something you can spray to make your boss go away. The hovercraft constantly looks over your shoulder, pesters you, and is always on your back. His expectations might be ridiculous, asking you, "Are you finished yet?" in an absurdly short period of time.

As difficult as it may be, you need to get space over this guy, or you'll go nuts. Be respectful, but forceful. Say something like this: "I may be the only one who feels this way, or I may be really strange, but it's hard for me to work my best when someone is looking over my shoulder. I'll tell you what. I guarantee you that if you'll give me three hours to work without any interruptions or questions, I'll have this thing finished and on your desk. And I think there's a pretty good chance you might even like it. If not, *then* we can discuss what needs to be changed."

This boss can be extremely annoying, but he is probably trying to be helpful. Most often, this boss will have a very anxious type of personality.

The best way to handle this boss is to go out of your way to keep him in the loop. Give him regular reports. Tell him five times as much as you think he needs to know and twice as frequently as you think you should.

Now that we've discussed how to handle various work personalities, let's take a few moments to discuss how you should treat yourself at work.

What You Wear at Work

Because of the day and age in which we live, I'm tempted to say that the most important thing you can wear to the office is a bra! With all the sexual harassment suits going on, there's more truth to that line than many of us would care to admit.

Regardless of the type of boss you have, your job is to build a strong team. That usually means being strong where your boss is weak. If your boss is unorganized, you must become ultraorganized. If your boss can't make decisions, you must learn how to help him make decisions.

Your first item of clothing, then, is *cooperation.* Women are unusually good at cooperation; men frequently have a much more difficult time working together. Your presence in the workplace can be invaluable if you can further hone and develop these team-building skills.

Another key issue throughout this chapter—and throughout the entire book—is the matter of respect. Here's where I answer the question posed to you in the very first chapter: the most important thing you can wear to the office is respect. You want to treat people with respect, but you also want to be treated with respect. Don't put yourself in a position where you'll be used all the time. Women aren't for using. If you're in an abusive work situation, do your utmost to find somewhere else to work.

Though men seem very tough on the outside, at the end of the day we're usually responders. You can often dictate how others treat you by how you *let* them treat you. I knew of one office where a guy we'll call "Dan" was a virtual tyrant. He wasn't the boss—and a case could be made that he wasn't even number two—but he acted as if everybody worked for him.

When a female colleague was hired who also reported directly to the boss, Dan tried to stake out his ground by telling her what she could or couldn't do and by belittling her. Dan had gotten away with doing this for his entire career, and he expected that the same would be true of Harriet. He was sadly mistaken.

Other women melted at the forcefulness of Dan's voice; Harriet would have none of it. She shot right back, "Dan, I will *not* allow you to talk to me that way or in that tone of voice. I am not a child, and I expect to be treated with respect."

Mouths dropped open as Dan wilted in front of everybody. For the first time in his life he seemed to be completely out of words. Nobody had ever called Dan's bluff before. He was the cowardly lion who had finally been found out.

It's not easy working in a world of men, but it's possible. And it's getting easier. Women have more advantages and opportunities today than ever before. In my home state (Arizona), the top five elected government officials are women.

Knowing your boss's or subordinates' birth order and working style—and adding to that knowledge the personal traits of cooperation and self-respect—will go a long way in helping you have a rewarding and successful vocational life.

Single Issues: Life As a Single or Newly Divorced Woman

Ten years ago you thought you had found the man of your dreams. What do you do when he becomes the man of your nightmares? Relating to a man who loves you and is committed to you for life is difficult enough. Relating to a man whom you've divorced and who considers you enemy number one may be the most challenging thing you ever do.

Expect tension. Most couples walk naively into marriage, but that doesn't surprise me nearly as much as the couples who walk naively into divorce. Think about it: if the two of you couldn't get along while you were married, what makes you think you'll be able to get along now that you're divorced and you introduce new wives, new husbands, new in-laws, and the competing demands of separate living arrangements and vacations into the equation? I've seen couples continue their disputes into divorce, and I've seen couples learn to get along. This chapter is designed to move you into the latter camp. Let's work toward civility and cooperation. Nobody wins when two people keep fighting. Even worse, the biggest losers are invariably the children.

In this situation *you must learn to avoid triangles.* Keep yourself out of the middle. First, avoid creating a triangle between your ex-husband and your kids. Second, avoid creating a triangle between your ex-husband and his new wife/girlfriend. Let's discuss each of these in order.

Ex-Husband Does Not Mean Ex-Father

Tommy rushes home from school, puts on his play clothes, grabs his mitt and bat, and waits eagerly by the door for his dad to pick him up. Your ex-husband has promised to take Tommy out to the baseball diamond to work on his hitting.

Three o'clock—the agreed-upon time—comes and goes, and Tommy gets anxious. At 3:30, Tommy starts to pout. At four o'clock, he starts picking on his sister. By 4:30, his anger has turned inward, and you find yourself feeling as angry as you've ever been. Not only has your ex torn your family apart, but by his irresponsibility and broken promises, he continues to make your life difficult.

As challenging as this may be, you must avoid becoming the third party and creating an unhealthy triangle for your children. For starters, *don't make excuses for your ex-husband.* When Tommy asks you why Daddy didn't show up, say, "I don't have a clue, but you know Dad's phone number. Why don't you give him a call and ask him?"

You must keep the tennis ball where it belongs—in your ex-husband's court. It's not your place to make excuses or to psychoanalyze your ex-husband. Keep the dispute between your ex and your kids.

Most divorced women already feel guilty about all their kids are going through, so they may try to cover up the ex's neglect and even cruelty, hoping to "soften" the blow. When you make excuses for your ex, your children will see through your weak explanations. They'll feel the sting of their father's unfaithfulness, and they'll have to deal with a mother's warped sense of justice. Just imagine how frightening it must be to discover that you can't trust Dad or Mom!

There's an equally troublesome problem. What if the ex-husband is a loser, and he wants access to the kids? As long as we're not talking about blatant abuse, you should give your ex-husband access to his children. Legally you're probably required to anyway. You're going to ask me, "But what if he lets them do things I don't? What if he takes them to R-rated movies or lets them eat all kinds of junk food?"

I'm sorry, but ultimately you have no control over what goes on in your ex's home. Some situations can't be fixed. If you married and made babies with a guy of low character, you and your kids are going to have to live with the consequences of that prior decision. Using the kids as pawns in a war against him will make things worse. Please don't do that to your children. This prohibition includes guerrilla warfare—bad-mouthing your ex to your children. It does no good whatsoever and can be quite harmful.

The best-case scenario of surviving a divorce (assuming that "best-case scenario" can *ever* be applied to a divorce) is modeled by a couple with whom I'm currently working. This man and woman have decided that the battles ended with the marriage. Both concentrate on treating each other with civility. They don't feign affection, but they speak respectfully of each other.

Most important, they back up each other's differences and roles in parenting. The man is rather volatile and very controlling (that's part of the reason why the woman divorced him), and the woman knows she can't change him. When one of her sons came up with a rather harebrained idea, she said, "Look, Johnny, you know your dad is never going to go for that, so why are you running it by me? You know your dad and I will have to sit down and discuss this, and when we do that, you know what he'll say."

The wife recognizes that this volatile and controlling man *still has authority over her children*, and that's very important. It is always better—as much as possible—to work with your ex rather than against him.

Working with your ex can be a vacation compared to working with a new wife or girlfriend.

The New Honey

The second triangle you must avoid is the one between your husband and his new wife or girlfriend. If you ever want a perfect setup for a catfight, you can't beat this one! You and the new honey are immediate and natural competitors. Even though you and your ex-husband couldn't stay married, at least you probably share a common interest in the welfare of your children. That's more than you and the new honey will ever have, so play the odds and *deal with your ex* as much as possible.

Your ex-husband (particularly if he's a weak man) may try to avoid confrontations by passing his battles with you onto his new girlfriend. You'll know this is taking place if you get a phone call that begins, "Frank wanted me to tell you that next time he picks up the kids, please have them ready on time."

Stop this conversation *immediately*. In a respectful, but firm, voice say, "Thank you, Sharon, for making this call. I know it wasn't easy.

But if Frank has something to say to me, please tell him to call me directly. I am not going to get involved in three-way conversations."

It's unlikely you'll be able to completely avoid the new woman. You'll undoubtedly find yourself in certain social situations and school events where your ex brings his new honey. There's no question that this can be an awkward situation, so here's my advice: if your ex is shacking up with someone, a high school basketball game is not the place to air your moral concerns. Choose a better venue. Don't take out your frustration with your ex on anyone else, even his new girlfriend.

> **Leman's Law #36:**
> You don't have to be friends with your ex's honey, but you do have to be polite.

You don't have to act like a dear friend, but for your kids' sake you must be civil, respectful, and polite. If it's a volatile situation and you truly don't believe you can avoid a blowup, then do everybody a favor and sit on the opposite side of the gym. If you really can't be polite, then avoidance is the next best option; do anything to avoid a confrontation that will embarrass your children.

A woman talked with me about a complicated triangle, one that was explosive. After bearing two children with her husband, this wife received the heartbreaking news that her husband was leaving her for another woman. She found out he had been conducting multiple affairs, and this one was taking him all the way into divorce court.

Once this guy married the new wife, however, he came back to wife number one and started proclaiming his love to her all over again. At first, she was excited.

"Do you want him back?" I asked.

"Of course, I do! We were meant for each other, and he's the father of my children."

Therapy can be really hard in these cases. I had to tell her to back off. "Don't you see that he's doing to his new wife the same thing he did to you, and you're being an accomplice?"

There was a long period of silence. "I guess I never looked at it that way."

"Your ex-husband always wants the forbidden. The reason you look good to him right now is that he can recapture the thrill of 'cheating' once again—this time doing it *with* you instead of *to* you."

"So what should I do?"

"Take ten steps back. You'll need to discuss the children's welfare, but any discussions about how he's not getting along with his new wife or how he wants to come back to you are entirely inappropriate. You shouldn't think about remarriage when he is already married to someone else."

> **Leman's Law #37:**
>
> Triangles always strangle. If you get involved in one of any kind, you're headed for disaster.

The cruelty of this man expresses itself on multiple levels. Not only did he break his first wife's heart by leaving her for another woman, but now he won't let her get on with her life. He wants to keep her on a string, allowing himself to enjoy a cheap, dirty thrill, once again at his first wife's expense. He's a total user, a man of whom any woman should be doubly wary.

Help! I'm a Single Mom Raising a Son (or Sons) by Myself

When a father is completely absent or distant, a mother may fall into the trap of trying to become a father. She tells herself, *I'd better go out and buy a baseball glove and a hockey stick and try to be the father this boy never had.*

That's an understandable approach, but a misguided one. You'll do nothing but create confusion if, as a mom, you try to act like a dad. The boy has lost one good role model; please don't take away the other one! Be a sterling mom; model what a woman is, how a woman thinks, the way a woman relates to males. If you enjoy sports, feel free to pass that love on to your boy, but don't do anything in such a way that you're trying to become something you're not. The truth is, you can't replace the father. No matter how often you play tackle football, no matter how many war movies you rent, no matter how many ball games you take him to, your son will still grieve the loss of his dad.

My second recommendation is that you stay single until the children grow up and leave the house (I write this knowing full well that most people will blow off this advice). I have worked with many blended families. Take my word for it: staying single is much easier in the long run. Families don't blend; they collide. Blending is a lie. The new parent will be a constant reminder of the child's loss, and there is nothing you can do to erase that. You'll also completely upset the dynamics of two families: there will be new rivalries, and established birth order patterns will get uprooted with rather messy results. For instance, imagine a firstborn being displaced by an older firstborn from the "new" family. You think the younger firstborn will gladly give way? Not on your life. It's equally unlikely that little lastborn Lucy will be enthused that Mommy or Daddy has a "new" baby in the family. The whole concept of blended families is a misnomer. It's more appropriate to talk about "blender" families because all you'll have is a liquid mess.

Like most single moms, if you insist on dating anyway, please don't bring Billy Boyfriend home. If you must date, do so *outside the home*. Don't let your child bond with an adult unless you are absolutely sure that the relationship is going to be lifelong. The child has already felt the pain of abandonment once. It is cruel to have the child bond with and watch two, three, or four boyfriends act nice to him and leave. All that does is compound the original feelings of betrayal. It's a great recipe to thoroughly destroy your son's self-image, confidence, and comfortableness with members of his own sex.

You must be careful here. All your feelings will urge you to introduce your boyfriend to your children as soon as possible. You're going to want to see how they do together. Your feelings will tell you, *This is the one! This is a keeper! I can't wait to tell the kids!* long before you've had a chance to adequately test the relationship.

At all costs, *resist these feelings*. Wait until they die down. Then after an offer of marriage has been made, you can begin the introductions.

If you do remarry, make sure he is a godly man. He *must* be a man who puts others' feelings before his own, who is tender and gentle, yet strong and caring. These requirements are precisely why I tell women to stay single; there are few men like this out there! Having a negative example from a stepfather is much more damaging than being raised by a single mom.

A lot of single men will act nice while they date you. They'll give you flowers, candy, and affection galore as part of their single-minded pursuit to hop into your pants, but once they have you, instead of finding another husband, you may find you've married another child who expects you to do his cooking, laundry, and baby-sit *his* kids while he plays golf with the boys.

If you're reading this and saying, "It's too late, Dr. Leman! I've already blown it! Now what do I do?" I sympathize with you. I've found it's helpful to hold regular "anger" meetings, where kids are encouraged to verbalize what they are angry about. You'll need the patience of Job and the wisdom of Solomon to keep these meetings from disintegrating into shouting matches, but bitter silence can be more destructive than open hostility.

Now, let's examine some information about looking for your new husband, whether you're single, divorced, or widowed.

The Keys to Freedom

"Honey, for you to be healed, you've got to look *inside*. You've got to get in touch with your feelings."

If you listen to this afternoon TV advice, you'll make an absolute mess of your life. The worst advice you can give to a woman—particularly one who has been negatively imprinted by her father (see Chapters 5 and 6)—is to follow her feelings. If you've already had one bad marriage, you need a strong wake-up call. After all, you followed your feelings into the first one, didn't you? Look where that got you! And if you continue to follow your feelings, you'll continue to pick the wrong man every time. At the end of your life, you'll be amazed that every one of your six husbands was *the same man*. Some had more hair than others; some had a leaner look; but inside, every one was exactly the same.

"Olivia," who is in her mid-forties, attended one of my seminars for singles. She stood up in front of the group when I asked for a volunteer who had suffered a really lousy marriage.

"Describe one of your parents, Olivia," I asked.

"My dad is . . ."

Olivia lapsed into a painful silence. Just before it became a little too awkward, she changed tactics and said, "Well, let me tell you about my mom. She's controlling, a high achiever, very bossy, and pushy."

Having gotten this out, she seemed ready to tackle her father. "My dad, well, let's just say he really messed up. He wasn't around much."

"All right," I told her in front of the group, "let me make a guess about your husband. He was a druggie, a loser, and an alcoholic."

"Go for it, Doc," Olivia laughed. "You're three for three."

Suffering from Daddy Attention Deficit Disorder (DADD) and being raised by a controlling mother virtually guaranteed that Olivia would bring home a "wounded dove," a weak person that she thought she had to fix, for a husband. Because her foundational "cake" was missing those all-important ingredients of a daddy's affirmation, acceptance, and presence, Olivia feels forced to prove her worth by achieving and by taking care of others. It didn't surprise me that for her vocation, she chose being a nurse in an intensive care unit.

Olivia is exactly the type of person—quick thinking, competent, empathetic, and trustworthy—you would want caring for you in a medical emergency. But brilliance in her profession can't overcome the ache in her soul over choosing the wrong men as husbands.

Unless Olivia makes a conscious intellectual shift, her feelings will always move her toward the wrong men. If she follows the advice she hears on television, she will exchange one wounded bird for another and never break out of the cycle of choosing losers.

She needs to learn to be like an NFL quarterback—someone who can line up, review the opposing defense, and choose a strategy that adapts to the new environment. Instead of always doing the predictable thing, she needs to look for ways to change.

If you've found yourself "suddenly single," whether from divorce or death, and you're concerned about getting back into the dating pool, I urge you to begin practicing the art of cognitive self-discipline.

Stop, Look, and Listen

The road to health isn't traveled via a rocket; it's a patient walk on a stairway with many little steps, one after the other. A woman needs to learn how to make a consistent series of choices that will set her free from her feelings. She needs to value long-term health over short-term relief.

This is never a once-and-for-all decision. It is more the case of taking three steps forward and two steps back. You'll revert to old habits. You may fall back into destructive behavior or thought patterns, but I hope you'll keep getting a little farther down the road so that when you fall back, you won't fall quite so far. It takes time to change.

I like to use the phrase "cognitive self-discipline" (CSD) to remind people that I'm a psychologist, but in reality, the best way to recover from a habit of choosing the wrong man is to remember these three words: *stop*, *look*, and *listen*. If you get these three steps down, you'll have mastered CSD.

CSD encourages you to get in touch with your brain, not your feelings. To remind yourself of why you need to do this, take a quick inventory of your past. When you've most blindly followed your feelings, what was the result? Did your feelings lead you into the promised land or—far more likely—the Sahara Desert?

If you're looking for Mr. Right, approach the man as you would an old, busy railway crossing. Stop, look, and listen before you proceed.

To stop means to put the feelings on hold long enough to look seriously at the man you're considering. Above all, it means *don't sleep with him until you're married.* Sexual intimacy will completely mess up your attempts to achieve an objective analysis of this guy.

As you're spending time with him, make a few mental notes. Remind yourself, *I might be a bit starved for attention these days and easily overwhelmed by the fact that somebody actually spent money on me or thinks I'm attractive. I need to be careful.*

Or it may go like this: *I so want the kids to have a good father, and Harry certainly seems to enjoy my kids. But have I known him long enough to be sure he would be a good father? Do I know him well enough to trust him with my daughters? Will he really be a good role model for my son?*

This will lead you into the second stage of CSD—look. Be honest. Don't think, *Yes, I know he's been divorced three times, but I really think he just never met the right woman. Besides, he took me out to an expensive restaurant, and I haven't had a date for two years! Nobody understood him before, but I understand him, and he'll change for me.*

If you're expecting a forty-five-year-old man to change, you'd better be a plastic surgeon, because it'll take a scalpel and a doctor's license to make this man look appreciably different five years down the road.

Honestly *look* at him. Not through the lens of your father (if that was a negative experience for you), but through the lens of what you *should* expect. What kind of family is he from? What's his attitude toward women? Is this a guy who enjoys telling filthy stories where the woman is always the brunt of the joke? Does he have a temper? (Be especially careful here.) How does he treat the key women in his life—his mother, grandmother, and sister?

Third, be willing to *listen*. What is God telling you? What do you really hear that man saying? Does he always have to be right? Is he giving any clues to a weakness that you'll ignore at your peril? When something goes wrong, is it always someone else's fault?

Listen for what I call the "uh-oh" phenomenon. Too many women have told me—much too late—"I walked down the wedding aisle knowing I probably shouldn't be doing this." They had heard that inner *uh-oh, be careful,* but they didn't listen to it. They didn't trust it enough to check it out.

If you can't trust your father, introduce the man to your pastor. Let a man—who isn't charmed by this Casanova—give you his honest opinion. Ask your girlfriends, "Am I blind to any of this man's faults?"

And then, *listen* to them. Even if you're sure they're wrong, don't respond immediately. Definitely *don't* attack or refute their analysis, even if every precious feeling in your body insists they are dead wrong. You must remind yourself that relying on your feelings got your life into such a mess in the first place. Realize that the negative imprint is working overtime to keep you responding inappropriately.

If you have given their input serious thought and made an honest analysis, and you're still convinced they are wrong, think it through again. If you're still positive they don't understand this man, go back to them and listen some more. If you can't convince them, be careful. Remind yourself that your pastor and/or your friends are objective observers with your best interests at heart. If you can't convince them of why this man is right for you, you're perilously close to making the same mistake one more time.

Use the brain God gave you to redirect the heart you long to give to a man. Mastering the art of CSD will require tremendous maturity and strength, but it will pay big dividends. If you *don't* do this, you'll wake up six months after your third marriage, beaten down one more time, once again telling yourself that you're no good.

The primary power of CSD is the power to say no. For many women, that's the most important word they'll ever learn to use, as you'll see in the next section.

Know the No Power

"Dr. Leman, we'd like you to appear on a panel for us again," Oprah's associate producer inquired (very early in the morning, I might add). "Think you could get on a plane today and come out to Chicago?"

"I don't think so," I replied. I have learned to avoid panels with a passion. You never get to fully express your perspective when five people appear at the same time, and I'm not interested in shouting over others to gain my thirty seconds of airtime.

Forty-five minutes later, Oprah's senior producer called me. "I understand that you have a problem with our associate producer, and you don't want to appear on the show."

"No, that's not true," I said. "I don't have any problem with that producer."

"Well, did you know we're the top-rated talk show?"

"Sure, I know that."

"Then why did you turn us down?"

"I don't do panels," I explained.

"Oh," she said.

Twenty minutes later the senior producer called back. "We decided to change the show."

"What's the change?" I asked.

"You're it."

I was on a plane that morning.

There can be tremendous power in the word *no*. Saying no can move you from a terrible situation to an ideal one. But you have to be willing to suffer a mini-loss if you want to get the real thing.

You'd better know who you are. For CSD to work, I want to see you—to put it bluntly—hold on to your pants and your top, say no to this guy whenever he wants to take a peek, and really get to know his character. Spend the time to see how he reacts in the summer *and* the winter. See if he begins taking you for granted or if his generosity wanes without a roll in the hay.

If your suitor wants you to mutually exercise each other's organs, let him know in no uncertain terms that the brain is the most intimate organ each of you has, and until the pastor says, "I now pronounce you husband and wife," that's the only organ he'll be exploring.

Every woman wants intimacy, but intimacy isn't found in the bedroom. It might be expressed there, but it's not created there. Intimacy is found in meaningful conversation. After the first instance of sexual relations, the intimacy level for the man goes *down*. He's thinking, *Now that I've gotten what I was after, why put in overtime on the relationship?* His primary goal has been met!

When a woman tells me, "He loves me," the first question I ask her is, "Are you sleeping with him?"

When she says, "Yes," I say, "You sound pretty sure of yourself. Do you want to put that to the test? Tell him you'd like to stop having sex, and see if his attitude toward you changes."

Why act like the majority of single women out there? Why not mark yourself as someone who is different and therefore special? If you agree (as many people do) to have sex on the second or third date—or anytime before marriage—odds are that the relationship won't make it. Respect needs to be built long before the marriage starts. While some women have told me they don't mind the thought of a sexually "experienced" husband, I have yet to meet a man who says he relishes the thought of a woman who has slept with numerous men. This thought usually terrifies a man or repulses him, and neither response helps your chances for a long-term commitment.

You have to be willing to say no to overcome the mistakes of the past. To find a suitable partner, you must travel through dangerous territory and steer around a number of potholes before you find the right man.

Just north of Tucson, where I live, is a state penitentiary. It's in the middle of a desert, and a highway runs past it. Prison officials have posted a sign that causes me to chuckle every time I see it: "State Penitentiary: Do Not Pick Up Hitchhikers."

Dating today is like traveling through a land populated by prisoners, rule breakers, and women haters. The challenge is to learn how to spot the winners without giving yourself away to the losers. Feelings don't know how to say no. Feelings want to run unhindered. For some reason, following your feelings will seem more romantic, but it's more like having a fling on the *Titanic*.

If you've had some glaring deficiencies in your background, you'd better become good at thinking things through. Otherwise, you'll end up feeling like a steel marble in a pinball machine, bounced back and forth unmercifully, sometimes clubbed, until you're not sure which end is up.

CSD empowers you to make expert use of the word *no*. This does far more than steer you toward the right man. Knowing the power of *no* transforms you into the right woman. Saying no makes you a respectable woman, and being a respectable woman draws a respectable man.

Remember, think long-term. Walk carefully, thoughtfully, deliberately, and safely, and you can slowly work your way into a healthy relationship with a man.

Questions About Men in General

In this chapter, we're going to address questions that frequently come up in my seminars and counseling sessions.

1. Why Do Men Look Down on Women?

This ugly historical reality has been true since God created us human beings. Reliable historians have yet to find a society that was ruled primarily by women. As I said before, this may change. But there's no escaping the fact that for thousands of years, this has been a man's world.

Some men see women as inferior because they are physically smaller. Sure, there are a few women who could pulverize many men in a boxing ring, but taken as a whole, women tend not to be as strong as men. Now that we're in the information age, the stress on physical strength is becoming less important. Consider the fact that the world's richest man is Bill Gates—hardly the poster child for brute physicality. The idea that physical strength equals worth is a ridiculous holdover from an outdated era when might made right.

A woman's emotional predisposition plays into this notion. Men think that aloofness and intellect are superior to emotions. Now, here again, you're going to find many women who are vastly more intelligent than most men, but I'm talking about our approach to solving problems and relating to others. It's far more common for men to take an analytical approach, and to many, this is synonymous with a superior approach.

Leman's Law #38:

Some men will never learn to respect women in general, but all men can learn to respect a specific woman if she earns it.

Compounding the issue in Christian circles, a number of men have, unfortunately, taken Paul's admonition, "Wives, submit to your own husbands," and translated this into a divinely ordained dictatorship. Although I believe there is a difference in sex roles, the Bible clearly does not ordain tyranny. The Scriptures urge men to love their wives as Christ loved the church—and Christ *died* for the church. We are called to be servant leaders.

Then we have to look at family of origin. Prejudice dies hard. Many men regard their wives as inferior because that's the attitude their fathers modeled. If a man is the sole wage earner, he might think of his wife as a dependent whom he has to support.

If one or any of these are true with the man you work with, live with, or listen to preach on Sunday morning, how should you respond?

First, you have to make your stock go up. You can't insist that men respect you attitudinally, but you can insist that men *treat you* with respect. To do this, don't allow yourself to be used. If you're in management with six men, there's no reason you should always get the coffee—provided you're all colleagues. Say, "You know what? I got the coffee last time. I think it's Scott's turn this time."

Your job in such situations isn't to change the minds of the men in question. You'll probably never do that. Some men will never learn to respect women in general, but—on the positive side—all men can learn to respect a specific woman if she earns it. You earn respect by hanging in there, being effective, being self-assured, *expecting* respect, and learning to communicate effectively.

2. Why Do Men Spend Money the Way They Do?

Women may spend enormous amounts of money on clothes, including things for the children, but men are apt to buy the really big items. If they're hunters, they won't think twice about dropping several hundred bucks for a new gun or eighty dollars for a new scope. If they own a boat, well, the old definition that a boat is a hole in the water through which you pour all your money isn't too far from the truth.

I heard a true story of a wife whose husband's dream was to buy a boat. He did so, at considerable expense, and took it out on the water *once*. After that, he parked it in the backyard. Several years later, the couple moved across state to a new house. Despite the wife's pleas, the husband insisted that the boat go with them, so they towed the boat to their new home and promptly parked it in the backyard.

The wife had learned her lesson, so she planted a huge bush right in front of the boat, hoping to block it from the house's view. Her plan worked. Seven years later (the boat had not left the yard once), the boat was almost completely covered. Then tragedy struck. The husband's best friend died, which was bad enough. Even worse, he left the woman's husband another boat, which the husband dutifully towed over to his house and parked in front of the bush!

I'll be the first to admit that it sometimes takes a tremendous amount of patience to live with a man. When you add money into the equation, you may need the virtues of a saint.

One time as I was interviewed on NBC, I said men regard money as a source of control. They tend to think, *I earned this and I'm going to spend it!* Women tend to regard money in a much more utilitarian way—that is, money is a tool you can use to buy things for others. Remind yourself that money is an issue of control with your husband, and you'll interject much more reason into your marriage.

> **Leman's Law #39:**
> Spending money is an issue of control; if your husband thinks you're trying to shortchange him with a tightfisted grab of the checkbook, he may spend more than he would have otherwise, just to exert his control.

I like to tell wives what I tell parents: choose your battles wisely. If you pick at every fifty- and sixty-dollar purchase that your husband makes, those purchases (and bigger ones) will tend to increase. It's only natural that you're thinking, *The money spent on that titanium driver would have paid for five pairs of shoes!* but marriage involves give-and-take. If you wanted absolute control over how every dime is spent, you should have stayed single. It is unreasonable to assume that your husband will run each expenditure by you. As difficult as it may be, learn to bite your tongue, admire the driver, and wait for a more appropriate time to mention that you really need a new clothes dryer more than he needs to drop his golf score by a few strokes (as if that would really happen anyway!).

By learning to choose your battles, you can step forward to stop your husband's worst excesses. When you know finances are really tight, approach your husband at a time and in such a way that it won't seem like an accusation: "Honey, what do you suggest I do to help us make the paycheck stretch out long enough to actually cover the entire month?" (But make sure this doesn't sound as if you're suggesting he doesn't earn enough—you must never forget what I said in Chapter 12 about the male ego!) When your husband sees you're really struggling, he might watch his own spending habits more closely.

Remember: pick your battles wisely. Your husband will listen to only so many complaints before he tunes you out.

3. What Is It About Men and Sports?

As "This Week's Sign That the Apocalypse Is Upon Us," the editors of *Sports Illustrated* once chose the $24.95 Stadium Pal, which is essentially a condom attached to a plastic bag that can be worn under the pants. Male football fans no longer have to leave their seats to urinate. (Hey, all that beer has to go *somewhere*.) The fact that someone would think of creating such an invention is proof enough that guys take their sports pretty seriously!

The advent of television has brought sports to every home, every day, virtually every hour of the day. ESPN got it all started with twenty-four-hour sports; now we can view ESPN 2 and ESPN Classic too. Apparently twenty-four hours a day aren't enough.

Wives often ask me, "Why do men like things like football?" It's a fair question. After all, I'm fifty-seven years old, and last Christmas all I wanted was a Buffalo Bills jersey. What's behind this fascination? Why would a grown man put a football jersey at the top of his wish list?

In part, football is a very physical game, and we men are very physical beings. We like the sense of competition. We love the sight and sound of a good, solid hit.

Sports provide a safe way for men to bond. We don't usually talk about the kids; we talk about the Cardinals or the Cowboys and immediately feel a kinship. Sports talk has the additional benefit of giving us a way to identify with other men. If you listen to sports talk radio at all, you'll soon notice the zealots who call in and identify so completely with their team that they use a personal pronoun: "*We're* going to beat the Dolphins, no doubt about it!"

Some of us think of sports as ways to connect with our youth, but in truth, most of us aren't thinking back to our glory days. We were lucky to make the team. It's funny that ex-professional athletes always seem to say they don't watch the game they used to play. Those of us who do watch tend to be the hacks who didn't do diddly when we were on the field. I remember one ex-football player explaining, "When I turn on a game, to me it looks like I'm watching twenty-two guys *at work.*"

Finally, sports provide a certain measure of excitement for men who tend to have routine days. Even an accountant gets tired of numbers. On the weekend, we can leave the office behind, forget about the bills, paint our bellies, put on silly hats, and scream like banshees. Or we can follow the exploits of Tiger Woods as he goes for another amazing win. Sports offer an escape, and as escapes go, sports tend to be relatively harmless. Believe me, as a therapist, I know that there are many worse ways for men to seek excitement and adrenaline than to watch other men compete!

4. Can You Explain the Mystery of Men and Their Friends?

Boy, I wish I had sold a book for every husband who has ever been accused by his wife of not having enough friends (or deep enough relationships). Let's get this out of the way real fast: if your husband has deep friendships, he's unusual. If he has several close friends, he's one in a million. Men tend to be more reserved in this area. Part of this goes back to our communication style. Remember, a woman, on average, speaks about three and one-half times the amount of words in any given day that a man does. When a man comes home from work, he *never* thinks, *What I wouldn't give for a good forty-five-minute chat*. He would probably much rather sit down in front of the television and watch some sports.

This phenomenon is so universal, you should expect it. A man doesn't like to talk as much as a woman does. Since his job may require him to talk all day long, he frequently seeks refuge in a prolonged period of silence at night. If you've always wondered why your husband is less than enthusiastic about going to an evening Bible study, you may not need to look any farther. If he's a Christian, his reluctance probably doesn't have anything to do with his lack of interest in spiritual things; it's just as likely that he's tired of talking and wants to spent a quiet evening at home.

Another thing you're going to have to get used to is that male friendships are different from female friendships. Don't use *your* ruler to measure your husband's relationships. A woman may have a single best friend and several close friends. You talk with your best friend on the phone, you go shopping with your best friend, you probably take the kids over to your best friend's house, and you may discuss your sex life with your best friend.

We men tend to be much more compartmentalized in our friendships. We have fishing buddies, sports buddies, hunting buddies, and golfing buddies. We have friendships at work, but we'd never think of inviting some of these friends to our homes on a weekend. Conversely, we may have weekend friends whom we'd never consider inviting out to lunch during the workweek.

But that's okay with us. Since our friendships aren't as exclusive, we tend not to get so easily offended if another friend is spending more time with a different friend. While a woman may work through this quite often ("Why did she go out to lunch with Susie and not *me?*"), this issue doesn't even register on a man's radar. Just because a man plays golf with someone doesn't mean that he expects to go fishing with him or to eat out with him.

This might look shallow to you. Hey, that's the way we are. Look at the positive side of this: it leaves our deepest relational needs to be met by our wives.

Epilogue

The Pesky Duck

I was having coffee with my wife at our home in Tucson, looking out through our French doors at the Santa Catalina Mountains. Suddenly something went whizzing by.

"What was that?" Sande asked.

"I don't know," I said, "but it looked like it landed in our backyard!"

I got up, coffee in hand, and opened the door. Much to my surprise, I saw a mallard duck floating in the swimming pool.

Keep in mind, we live in a desert. You don't see a lot of ducks around our house. In fact, you don't see *any* ducks around our house.

"Honey, come here and look at this," I said. "We've got a duck in our pool."

"That's impossible!" Sande said.

I started chuckling.

"What's so funny?" Sande asked.

"I just can't believe a duck could come out of the middle of a desert and end up in our pool."

"Well, get him out of it before he uses the pool for a toilet!"

I walked toward the pool, assuming my presence would scare the duck away, but he nonchalantly floated to the other side of the pool, occasionally dipping his beak in the water and wetting his back as if I was nothing more than a minor nuisance.

I got more determined and started flapping my arms. "Okay, duck," I said as forcefully as possible, "move along. Shoo! Shoo!"

That duck didn't blink. The more cynical side of me thought I detected him laughing, but I freely admit that might be pushing it a bit.

"Can't you get him out?" Sande asked.

"You'll have to excuse me, Honey," I explained patiently. "But I've never had to move a duck before. I've studied adolescents, but never birds. I'm not quite sure what to do."

I could've sworn I heard Sande mutter, "Some psychologist you are!" but she denies saying that to this day.

Finally I gave up. "Honey," I said, "I'm sure this duck will be gone by nightfall. Let's just leave it alone for now."

"But the pool will be messy!"

"If the pool gets messy, I'll use the skimmer and clean it up."

Later that day, when the kids came home from school, they were as fascinated by that duck as I was. It became quite the conversation piece at our dinner table.

The next morning I woke up and immediately checked the backyard.

That blasted duck was still there!

Sande, my little Martha Stewart, decided that she had had enough. She was going to get rid of that duck one way or another, so she picked up the phone.

"Who are you going to call?" I asked dumbfounded. "The duck exterminator?"

Not quite. She reached the Loews Ventana Canyon Resort, a posh club located a couple of miles above our home.

"This is Sande Leman calling," she said. "We have one of your ducks at our home."

I just about fell over from laughing.

"Excuse me, ma'am?" the operator asked her.

"We have one of your ducks at our home."

"You have one of our ducks *in your home?*"

"Actually it's in our pool, and we want you to get it out of there before it makes a mess."

"Ma'am, how do you know it's one of our ducks?"

"It has to be," Sande said with firm conviction. "Where else could the duck come from?"

"Well, there are some man-made lagoons around here. I suppose it's possible a duck could live there."

"Fine," Sande said. "Let me talk with security."

Sande was transferred to security. I was picturing a twenty-year Marine Corps vet on the other line.

"Yes, this is Sande Leman, and we have one of your ducks . . ."

I could just imagine the conversation on the other line, with the security guy saying, "Excuse me, ma'am," putting his hand over the phone and yelling out, "Hey, Charlie, pick up extension three. I've got a live one! She says she's got one of our ducks!"

"What exactly is this duck doing, ma'am?"

"He's paddling around the pool. It has to be your duck, and we want it out of there!"

"You mean, you want me to drive over to your house, capture the duck, and bring it back to our resort?"

"Of course," Sande said. "It's *your* duck after all, and it's making a mess in our pool."

By that time, I was rolling on the floor laughing, and I'll bet you the security guy was too. Though Sande was all business, I'm sure the security guy was getting a big kick out of the conversation. Sande probably made his day!

After the guy had had his fun, he finally said, "Well, ma'am, if it *is* our duck, I'm sure he'll come home."

That sounded sensible enough to Sande. In her little cheery voice she chirped, "Well, thank you very much."

She put the phone down with a triumphant gesture and a self-satisfied smile on her face as if she had really accomplished something.

"Do you realize what that guy must be saying?" I asked her. "He's probably gathering everyone around him to tell the story even as we speak!"

I would never do what my wife did. For starters, how she connected that duck with the resort is beyond me, but she believed it with such certainty that it was hard to doubt her.

I'm sure you've experienced this with your husband. You've watched him do something and thought to yourself, *What in the world would make him do a thing like that?*

The truth is, we men and women may never understand each other. There will always be an element of mystery and the occasional shock. I've been married to Sande for more than thirty years, and her phone call *still* caught me by surprise!

But I hope this book has moved you a little farther down the road of understanding. I trust that understanding how life was for your husband when he was just a boy; how his ego drives much of what he does; how sex is never very far from his mind; and how he often really wants to please you but just plain doesn't know what to do will help you appreciate your spouse a little bit more.

He might be a mystery, but he's *your* mystery.

Enjoy!

Notes

Chapter 1

1. Barna Research Online, "Christians Are More Likely to Experience Divorce Than Are Non-Christians," 21 December 1999, <www.barna.org>.
2. Ann Landers, "Affair Leads to Divorce," *Bellingham Herald*, 31 March 1999, C2.
3. No author cited, "Blotter," *Sports Illustrated*, 13 December 1999, 28.
4. Michael Gurian, *The Wonder of Boys*, cited in Lynn Johnson, "Parenting: Babies and Toddlers," <www.About.com>.
5. Paul Candon, "Brain Structure May Influence Male-Female Behavior Differences," New York Times Syndicate <http://nytsyn.com>, 15 December 1999.
6. Jane Everhart, "Male, Female Differences Can Impact Treatment Regimens," New York Times Syndicate, 28 December 1999.
7. Ibid.
8. Dr. Lena Sun, "Gender Differences in Pain Sensitivity and Responses to Analgesia," *Journal of Gender-Specific Medicine*, 1 (1998), 28–30.
9. Everhart, "Male, Female Differences."
10. Dr. Sandra R. Leiblum, "Sexual Problems and Dysfunction: Epidemiology, Classification, and Risk Factors," *Journal of Gender-Specific Medicine*, 2 (1999), 41–45.
11. Cited in Leiblum, "Sexual Problems and Dysfunction," 41–45.
12. Leiblum, "Sexual Problems and Dysfunction," 41–45.

Chapter 2

1. Kathleen Parker, "Study Boys? Who Cares About Boys?" *Bellingham Herald*, 22 December 1999, A11.
2. For more on this topic, I recommend my book *Making Children Mind Without Losing Yours.* In this book, I introduce the idea of reality discipline, which is far more effective than setting rules.

Chapter 3

1. Dr. Archibald Hart, *The Sexual Man* (Dallas: Word, 1994), 119.
2. For an excellent discussion of this, on which much of what I write here is based, see Hart, *Sexual Man*, 42 ff.
3. Hart, *Sexual Man*, 46.
4. Cited in Hart, *Sexual Man*, 101. Ann Landers reversed her opinion in a later column.

Chapter 5

1. David Blankenhorn, "The Good Family Man," Children Youth and Families Consortium Electronic Clearinghouse, <www.cyfc.umn.edu>.
2. Walter Chan, "The Hysterical Spouse," *Medical Aspects of Human Sexuality*, 9 September 1985, 123–33.

Chapter 6

1. Cited in Gary Thomas, "The Forgiveness Factor," *Christianity Today*, 10 January 2000, 38.
2. Sue Kidd, "Don't Let It End This Way," reprinted in *Focus on the Family*, January 1985.

Chapter 8

1. Jean Kerr, *The Snake Has All the Lines*, "The Ten Worst Things About a Man" (1958), cited on Microsoft Bookshelf 99 and taken from *The Columbia Dictionary of Quotations*, licensed from Columbia University Press. Copyright © 1993, 1995, 1997, 1998 by Columbia University Press.
2. Gary Thomas, *Sacred Marriage* (Grand Rapids: Zondervan, 2000), 61.

Chapter 9

1. Hart, *Sexual Man*, 4.
2. Ibid., 5.
3. Ibid.
4. Ibid., 6.

Chapter 10

1. Hart, *Sexual Man*, 13.
2. St. Francis de Sales, *Thy Will Be Done: Letters to Persons in the World* (Manchester, NH: Sophia Institute Press, 1995), 7.
3. Christina Ianzito, "Not Tonight, Honey," *Capital Style*, August 1999.
4. Eric Schlosser, "The Business of Pornography," *U.S. News & World Report*, 10 February 1997, 44.

Chapter 12

1. Richard Hoffer, "A Lot More Than Lip Service," *Sports Illustrated*, 29 November 1999, 87.
2. Peter King, "Sinking Fast," *Sports Illustrated*, 29 November 1999, 140.
3. Joanne Kaufman, "Let's *Not* Talk About Sex," *Redbook*, October 1999, 104.

About the Author

Dr. Kevin Leman is an internationally known Christian psychologist, author, radio and television personality, and speaker. He has ministered to and entertained audiences around the world with his wit and common-sense psychology.

Leman cohosts the nationally syndicated program *RealFAMILIES.com* and has written more than twenty books on marriage and family. His books include the bestsellers *The New Birth Order Book*, *Sex Begins in the Kitchen*, and *Making Children Mind Without Losing Yours*, as well as *What a Difference a Daddy Makes*, *Bringing Up Kids Without Tearing Them Down*, and *Living in a Step-family Without Getting Stepped On*.

He is also a regular guest on national television talk shows, including *Oprah*, *Good Morning America*, *Live with Regis Philbin*, *CNN*, *The View*, CBS's *The Early Show*, and the *Today Show*. He is also heard frequently on Dr. James Dobson's *Focus on the Family* radio program.

Dr. Leman is the founder and president of Couples of Promise, an organization committed to helping couples remain happily married.

Leman attended North Park College. He received his bachelor's degree in psychology from the University of Arizona, where he later earned his master's and doctorate degrees. He and his wife, Sande, live in Tucson, Arizona. They have five children—Holly, Krissy, Kevin II, Hannah, and Lauren.

For additional resources or for seminar information, please contact:

Dr. Kevin Leman
Couples of Promise
P.O. Box 35370
Tucson, AZ 85740
Phone: (520) 797-3830
Web site: www.realfamilies.com

Don't Miss This Book by Kevin Leman

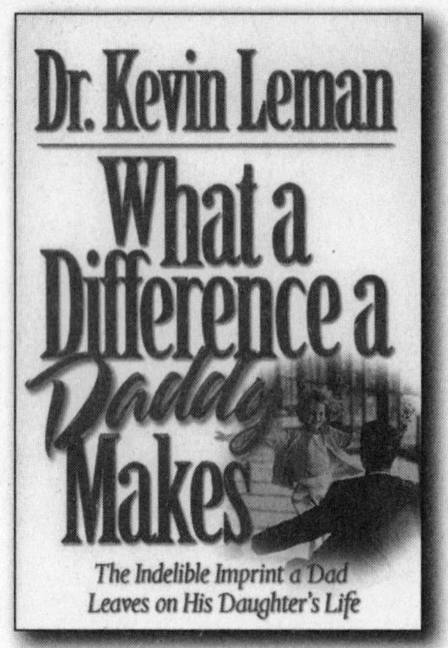

What a Difference a Daddy Makes

Study after study shows that fathers set up their daughters for success. Involved fathers—whether or not they live in the same house as their children—boost their daughters' academic achievement, promote their psychological health, increase their compassion for others, and even bolster the status of women.

What a Difference a Daddy Makes examines the characteristics of a healthy
er-daughter relationship. Dr. Kevin Leman seamlessly weaves the latest
on effective fathering with funny, moving stories about his own par-
riences. He outlines the architecture of the father-daughter rela-
ing how to build it on a foundation of trust. A father makes
ure by being consistent, Leman says.
this book will give dads hope. They'll read about what
r. Leman's and other fathers' families. His prac-
ways they can love their daughter, setting her
dult who can focus on loving others.

-2 • **Hardcover • 256 pages**

)4-6 • **Trade Paper • 256 pages**